The One Property Retirement

A Simple Strategy for Building Your Nest Egg

By: Jack Duffley

ISBN: 9798675027095 (paperback)

LCCN: 2020915788 (paperback)

First Edition 2020

Jack Duffley
P.O. Box 60028
Chicago, IL 60660

www.jackduffley.com

Download the Free Bonuses

Thanks for purchasing my book! To get access to all of the free stuff listed below, visit https://www.jackduffley.com/oprbook/.

- Rental Property Metrics Calculator
- Budgeting Spreadsheet
- Real Estate Metrics Cheatsheet

I also am a real estate agent in the Chicagoland area. If you are wanting to buy a property there, I'd be happy to help you, whether you are a complete beginner to real estate or a seasoned veteran. You can reach out to me directly by visiting http://jackduffleyagent.com/.

I'd greatly appreciate it if you left a review on Amazon! Your feedback will help others to discover this book and begin their paths towards building wealth in real estate.

Table of Contents

Introduction

After I graduated high school, I worked at a local credit union in the mortgage processing department. I was not particularly interested in real estate at that point, but I just so happened to have a friend's mom who worked there and gave me a chance to join the team after she put the good word in to the team's manager. Just a couple weeks out of high school, still blind to most of the financial world, I had my first real job.

One day that summer, a person from the financial planning team presented in front of all of the interns at the firm to teach them about retirement planning. He was in the middle of explaining how much we all needed to save in order to retire when he showed us a retirement calculator and flashed a very big number at us:

$1,000,000

If we wanted to retire in our 60s, he explained, we each would need to save something around $1,000,000 in order to have a comfortable retirement where we could withdraw a bit over a median salary without running out of money too quickly.

The fifteen, or so, of us interns gasped in horror. We were busy making $12 an hour and preparing to unload most of our summer savings on textbooks for school in the fall. How on Earth would we reach that number?

Like many of the others in the room, I was doing the ballpark math in my head and frustratingly realizing that a person would have to devote a massive portion of his or her salary exclusively towards retirement to meet this goal, even on a respectable income. And that was before paying any other debt or expenses, or, well, having a life.

There has to be a better way, 18-year-old me frantically thought for the rest of the summer. I began searching for an answer, a solution to this strange problem. Do most people even achieve this? Are they happy in trying to achieve it? What do rich people do to get ahead of the rest of the pack?

I ripped through books. I dove into many blog articles. I listened to hundreds of hours of podcasts. And a lot of them pointed to the same answer: real estate.

But the current retirement system for the vast majority of people ignores real estate. Homeowners might be able to build some equity over time, but the system constantly encourages people to refinance and routinely reset their amortization schedules, so many do not ever build substantial wealth as they might have expected. And even then, most people do not want to sell their home so that they can retire off of the proceeds, because, well, that's their home. And most people move around a few times in their lives, selling their home each time, resetting the amortization clock again.

How can someone incorporate real estate into a retirement plan? Thankfully, one does not need to become a mogul to reap the massive benefits of real estate. If a person plays his or her cards right, a one property strategy can do just fine, freeing up a massive amount of time and resources over the long run.

This book is divided into three parts. Part One goes over the traditional world of retirement planning and how inefficient it is. Part Two explains the one property strategy and how to save for retirement with drastically less effort than the traditional system. Part Three looks at how the one property strategy can be used as a springboard into other types of investing and looks at potential ways to fully capitalize on such a strong position.

I. Traditional Retirement Savings

Before we look at the one property strategy, it's important to understand what the current norms of retirement are. You may already be contributing to one of the "normal" plans now. Or maybe you have heard other people talk about their strategies. Understanding these approaches will help to conceptualize the benefits of the one property strategy in the coming chapters.

1. The Old World of Retirement

Traditionally, retirement plans were provided by a person's employer. That person would work for a company for a certain number of years, and then would get a pension until they died, which typically was only for a few years. After all, back in the 1930s, 40s, and 50s, life expectancy in the United States was only about 60 to 65 years of age. So, companies could more easily afford to take care of their retirees with their relatively short retirements. Current workers could pay into the pension system that would sufficiently cover the retired workers, who generally would not live much longer.

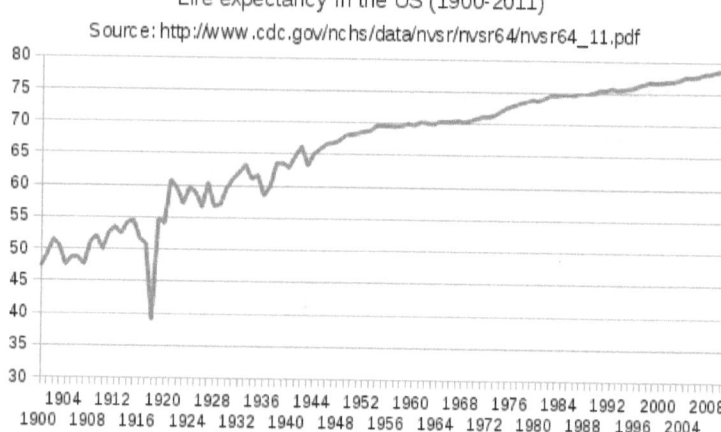

Life expectancy in the US (1900-2011)
Source: http://www.cdc.gov/nchs/data/nvsr/nvsr64/nvsr64_11.pdf

Life expectancy is significantly higher now. On average, people in the United States live to almost 80 years of age. That's a lot of extra years of retirement, and a lot of extra years of expenses!

More importantly, a demographic inversion is taking place. Although people are living longer, they generally are not having as many kids as previous generations. A population pyramid would ideally have more young people than old people. This would imply steady population and thus economic growth, with a large work force that can easily take care of the retired work force. As an example, here is the population pyramid in the United States from 1950:

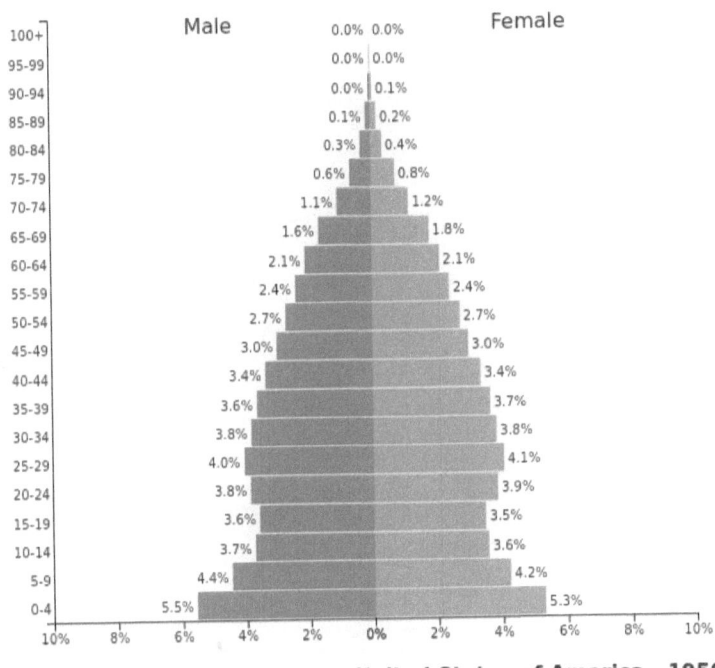

United States of America - 1950
Population: **158,804,396**

Notice how the population generally is mostly younger, working age people and tails off fairly quickly as the population gets older. This makes it easy to provide welfare services and pensions to seniors while the larger working

15

population supports them. But look at what happened over the next 60 years:

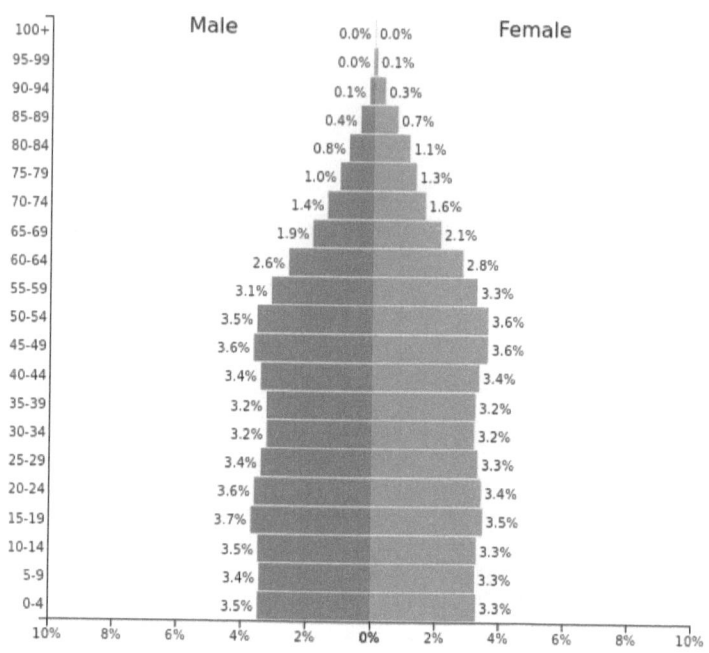

United States of America - 2010
Population: **309,011,469**

Compared to 1950, this population pyramid looks much more uniform, and only begins to tail off at around age 60, and it also has many more people living in their late 80s and early 90s. There are not significantly more young people than old people, and there actually is a sort of "bump" in the middle

16

age range where 45 to 50-year olds make up the plurality of the population. In short, there are not enough young people to support the aging population, and the problem will only become worse as the demographic inversion continues to worsen in much of the developed world.

What does this mean for the current working-class people who obviously hope to one day retire themselves? Simply put, pensions will probably not be an option. There will not be a sizable enough work force to support an increasingly "top heavy" population. This goes for programs like Social Security as well, where older retirees have to rely on younger workers to fund their increasingly long retirements. Something is going to have to give in the coming years, since the traditional retirement system is becoming increasingly unsustainable.

Thankfully, there are alternatives to the rather ancient pension system. As this demographic inversion has continued, and as pension systems have been severely limited outside of some municipal workers with powerful unions and politicians supporting them, people have looked elsewhere in preparing for retirement. Mutual funds have dominated many peoples' retirement plans in recent decades.

2. The Mutual Fund Era - IRAs and 401(k)s

Mutual funds are conglomerations of many different shares of stock that people can buy into to create a well-diversified portfolio with little time and effort. Index funds are an increasingly popular form of mutual fund that allow investors to quickly follow a broader index, like the S&P 500 or the Dow Jones Industrial Average. They can give even greater diversification with historically consistent results. They are often incredibly cheap compared to actively managed funds as well. Even actively managed funds may invest in index funds.

Many people now rely very, very heavily on the stock market in funding their retirement. Long term investors will be quick to point out that the stock market has returned about 7 percent per year on average, so investing in it for retirement makes sense for fairly stable *long-term* returns. It allows someone to take the dollar he or she earned today and multiply it many times over before being withdrawn many years down the line.

The government wants to encourage people to save for retirement as well. This is why it allows significant tax advantages through things like IRAs and 401(k)s. An IRA is an Individual

Retirement Account, while a 401(k) is an employer sponsored retirement plan with many of the same benefits as an IRA.

Both IRAs and 401(k)s come in two flavors: traditional and Roth. Roth accounts allow you to use post-tax money to invest in various assets, including stocks, and then you never have to pay any taxes on any gains. With traditional accounts, you get a tax deduction for the year you make your contributions, but then you have to pay taxes on your eventual withdrawals (including any gains) at your income tax rate.

Here's a look at the main differences, as of 2020, between these popular types of retirement accounts:

	Traditional		Roth	
Type:	IRA	401(k)	IRA	401(k)
Annual Contribution Limit:	$6,000; or $7,000 for those 50 years old and older	$19,500; or $26,000 for those 50 years old and older	$6,000; or $7,000 for those 50 years old and older	$19,500; or $26,000 for those 50 years old and older
Withdrawal Age:	59.5 years old for all gains and contributions without penalty	59.5 years old for all gains and contributions without penalty	59.5 years old for all gains without penalty; contributions can be withdrawn without penalty	59.5 years old for all gains without penalty; contributions can be withdrawn without penalty
Penalties:	Money withdrawn before 59.5 is added to gross income (and taxed accordingly) plus a 10 percent penalty in most situations.	Money withdrawn before 59.5 is added to gross income (and taxed accordingly) plus a 10 percent penalty in most situations.	Accrued gains withdrawn before 59.5 are added to gross income (and taxed accordingly) plus a 10 percent penalty in most situations.	Accrued gains withdrawn before 59.5 are added to gross income (and taxed accordingly) plus a 10 percent penalty in most situations.

There are some other types of retirement accounts as well, such as SEP IRAs or 403(b)s. All of them generally serve the same purpose of providing tax benefits while you invest for retirement.

20

With most retirement accounts, you might be forced to make minimum withdrawals from them by the time you are 70.5 years old, or else you will have to pay a steep penalty.[1] This is definitely the case with traditional accounts, but currently does not affect Roth accounts. That does take away some flexibility, but the benefits can be lucrative depending on your tax bracket.

Regardless, the way that most retirement accounts are set up make it very hard to invest in things besides stocks and stock funds. Contribution limits are not super high, so the benefits are naturally limited as well. Most importantly, a lot of your money is "trapped" within the account until you reach legal retirement age, and you will probably have to pay a penalty to remove much of that money if you want to do it sooner.

The contribution limits for IRAs, especially, make it tough to invest in more capital-intensive assets like real estate since you are very unlikely to be allowed to get a mortgage within it. And

---

[1] Internal Revenue Service. *Retirement Topics — Required Minimum Distributions (RMDs)*. https://www.irs.gov/retirement-plans/plan-participant-employee/retirement-topics-required-minimum-distributions-rmds

employer sponsored 401(k)s sometimes only invest in a broad mix of stocks and bonds, not real estate, although some do offer REIT (real estate investment trust) funds.

In short, most retirement accounts are biased to favor slow and steady stock investing, particularly through mutual funds. This makes it tough to unlock a lot of potential that comes with things like real estate investment and using debt to invest over the long term. However, this is not to say that you cannot retire on stock investing. The problem is that it will likely take a very long time and a ton of your hard-earned money. Let's take a look at how this is so.

3. Retiring on 7 Percent Returns

Let's say you are a reasonably diligent 25-year-old, and you want to start investing for your retirement. You like your job and it pays you a modest $40,000 per year. Although you have some student loan debt, you still aggressively save for retirement and max out your IRA at $6,000 per year and contribute to your 401(k) up to your employer match, which happens to be a 50% contribution match on the first 10% of your salary. So, you put $4,000 into your 401(k), and your employer matches with an additional $2,000. In sum, you are putting $12,000 towards your IRA and 401(k) combined every year.

You do this for 30 years. In the interest of keeping things clear, I will not include inflation in your salary or in your investments. The stock market has historically returned 7 percent on average after accounting for inflation. While your IRA is entirely made up of diversified stock index funds and does give you that 7 percent return, your 401(k) is a 60/40 split between stocks and bonds, so it returns you only 4 percent on average each year. Unless you switch employers, there is not much you can do here to change your 401(k) allocations. But they do give you a fairly generous match, at least!

Let's take a look at your account balances over those 30 years, and see where you will be as you near retirement age:

Year	Cumulative IRA Contributions	IRA Balance	Cumulative 401k Contributions	401k Balance	Total Cumulative Contributions	Total Retirement Balance
1	$6,000.00	$6,435.05	$6,000.00	$6,244.86	$12,000.00	$12,679.91
2	$12,000.00	$13,336.69	$12,000.00	$12,744.59	$24,000.00	$26,081.28
3	$18,000.00	$20,738.76	$18,000.00	$19,509.57	$36,000.00	$40,248.33
4	$24,000.00	$28,677.54	$24,000.00	$26,550.63	$48,000.00	$55,228.17
5	$30,000.00	$37,191.94	$30,000.00	$33,879.05	$60,000.00	$71,070.99
6	$36,000.00	$46,323.71	$36,000.00	$41,506.54	$72,000.00	$87,830.26
7	$42,000.00	$56,117.61	$42,000.00	$49,445.32	$84,000.00	$105,562.93
8	$48,000.00	$66,621.65	$48,000.00	$57,708.09	$96,000.00	$124,329.74
9	$54,000.00	$77,887.31	$54,000.00	$66,308.07	$108,000.00	$144,195.38
10	$60,000.00	$89,969.83	$60,000.00	$75,259.01	$120,000.00	$165,228.84
11	$66,000.00	$102,928.42	$66,000.00	$84,575.26	$132,000.00	$187,503.68
12	$72,000.00	$116,826.63	$72,000.00	$94,271.70	$144,000.00	$211,098.33
13	$78,000.00	$131,732.56	$78,000.00	$104,363.87	$156,000.00	$236,096.43
14	$84,000.00	$147,719.30	$84,000.00	$114,867.91	$168,000.00	$262,587.20
15	$90,000.00	$164,865.20	$90,000.00	$125,800.62	$180,000.00	$290,665.82
16	$96,000.00	$183,254.33	$96,000.00	$137,179.50	$192,000.00	$320,433.83
17	$102,000.00	$202,976.82	$102,000.00	$149,022.77	$204,000.00	$351,999.59
18	$108,000.00	$224,129.35	$108,000.00	$161,349.37	$216,000.00	$385,478.72
19	$114,000.00	$246,815.61	$114,000.00	$174,179.03	$228,000.00	$420,994.63
20	$120,000.00	$271,146.81	$120,000.00	$187,532.27	$240,000.00	$458,679.08
21	$126,000.00	$297,242.22	$126,000.00	$201,430.47	$252,000.00	$498,672.69
22	$132,000.00	$325,229.76	$132,000.00	$215,895.87	$264,000.00	$541,125.63
23	$138,000.00	$355,246.63	$138,000.00	$230,951.61	$276,000.00	$586,198.24
24	$144,000.00	$387,439.96	$144,000.00	$246,621.79	$288,000.00	$634,061.76
25	$150,000.00	$421,967.58	$150,000.00	$262,931.48	$300,000.00	$684,899.06
26	$156,000.00	$458,998.73	$156,000.00	$279,906.79	$312,000.00	$738,905.52
27	$162,000.00	$498,714.94	$162,000.00	$297,574.86	$324,000.00	$796,289.80
28	$168,000.00	$541,310.90	$168,000.00	$315,963.99	$336,000.00	$857,274.89
29	$174,000.00	$586,995.42	$174,000.00	$335,103.59	$348,000.00	$922,099.01
30	$180,000.00	$635,992.44	$180,000.00	$355,024.29	**$360,000.00**	**$991,016.73**

Looks like you reached your million-dollar retirement on a $40,000 salary! Great job! But, man, that was a lot of work, 30 years of hard work at your job, grinding towards this goal. After all, a quarter of your base salary was going towards your retirement, meaning you could not use that money for other things, like pursuing a passion, taking care of your family, or starting your own business.

You had to fork over $360,000 throughout those years just to get to a decently comfortable retirement (remember, this is in today's dollars, since this model does not factor in any inflation). That's quite a lot of money! And this is assuming you start in your twenties; if you waited to start investing for your retirement until your thirties or forties, you will have to contribute even more to reach the same number by retirement age.

This is a good time to explain that I do not denounce this approach to retirement in itself. It works for many people. It just takes an enormous amount of time and effort for the vast majority of those folks. And we only have so much time and effort to give as humans on this planet. If time is something you care about, it makes sense to look at other options as well. It's also important to understand any flaws with a particular approach.

4. The Problem with Getting Too Aggressive

OK, maybe that employer's 401(k) was too conservative, and you actually have a 401(k) that nets a greater average annual return because it is less heavily skewed towards bonds.

If that's the case, you may reach your million-dollar threshold more quickly, but you will be at much greater risk. Even if your more equity-focused portfolio might be up 20 percent in one year, it might plummet in the next, with far greater range in either direction than a portfolio with more bonds.

Stocks and bonds, like all other investments, closely follow the risk versus reward trade off. Taking on assets with higher expected returns is a double-edged sword. The higher your expected return (i.e., the more stocks over bonds) the greater your risk. Your investment may swing way more violently in either direction. This is not really a problem while you are saving for a retirement that's many years away, at least most of the time. However, this definitely can be a big issue if you are nearing retirement.

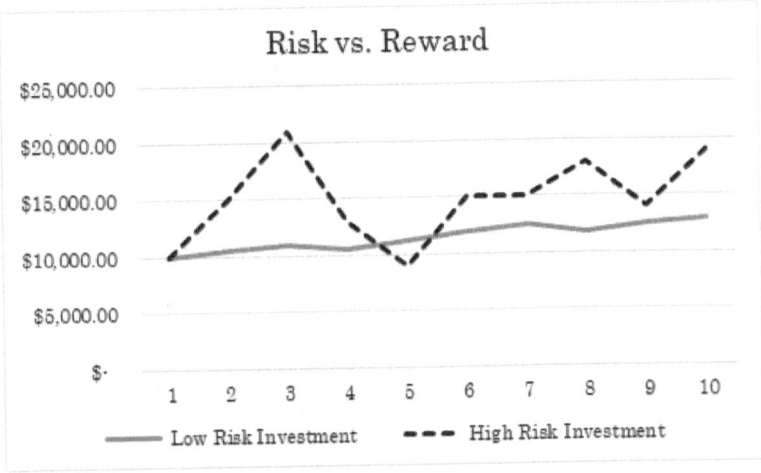

Risk vs. Reward

This chart illustrates how a higher risk investment might compare to a lower risk one over a 10-year period. Notice how much more volatile the higher risk investment is, with a much higher ceiling and floor. Over the long-term, we would expect the higher risk investment to yield a greater return than the lower risk one. But the lower risk one is drastically more stable in the near term. The lower risk one also has much less of a chance of spectacularly failing and going to zero.

Now imagine that you were approaching retirement with the higher risk investment in year 3 on the chart above. Just before you planned on retiring, your investment loses most of its value in years 4 and 5. If you let it ride out, you might be able to recover the losses. But you might not have the time to do that.

For example, in March 2020, the U.S. stock market plummeted approximately 20% due to uncertainty around the Coronavirus outbreak and the COVID-19 pandemic. For someone, say, a year from retirement who had mostly stocks, their assets were slashed in what probably felt like the blink of an eye. All of those years of higher returns in the previous decade were cut short by one terrible month. For someone wanting to rely on his or her account balance in the near future, this can spell disaster. You may really want to start withdrawing from that account very soon and might not have the years you need to allow that investment to recover.

No matter what position you take initially, it's likely that you will want to switch towards more bonds and less stocks within your IRA or 401(k) as you approach retirement. Your investment horizon will become increasingly short, and higher reward assets have much greater short-term volatility, so you will naturally want to move out of them if you are trying to live off of those funds. While taking a maximally aggressive approach early on might make sense due to having more years to make up any short-term losses, those years quickly fade away as you approach retirement. Simply put, you have less room for error the more that time passes. Thus, it's probably more than a tad ambitious to rely solely on equities or other higher risk assets, at least as you near the beginning of your planned retirement.

And, realistically, you probably are not going to have a 401(k) that is all equities. Many companies offer a limited number of plans that have to appease a broad array of employees at very different stages of their lives. Even if it is a more aggressive portfolio, high fees on the 401(k) plan might take away a lot of potential returns. However, some more comprehensive 401(k) plans do offer a broader array of stock versus bond ratios. If you are fortunate enough to have that kind of flexibility in your offered 401(k)s, you have much greater flexibility than many others.

Portfolio allocation can shave off years of getting towards your retirement number, but it can also *add* years if you are too aggressively positioned during a market dip near your retirement. Timing the market is nearly impossible to do with any reliability, so there is not much of a work around in this case if you are solely relying on stocks and bonds. But what happens when you actually reach your million and you are ready to ride off into the sunset?

5. Getting Through Retirement

One million dollars is a lot of money in itself. But how comfortable of a retirement can you possibly have on a million bucks?

Even when you reach your million-dollar retirement fund, you still will have quite a long way to go. If you retire at 60 years old, you can reasonably assume that you will live for at least 15 to 25 more years depending on your health. That's actually another challenge—there's no way of telling how much longer you will live. It follows that there's no way of telling how much money you will need to reserve for future years.

But even if you knew exactly how much longer you had to live, let's say 20 more years, you still are not going to have a particularly lavish retirement. If you move all of your retirement fund into more conservative assets like bonds that still protect principal against inflation, you would be able to withdraw about $50,000 per year. But if you live 1 extra year, well, it looks like you're going to have to start looking for work in your eighties.

Is that right? One million bucks is only $50,000 per year for a 20-year long retirement? If you keep that money in a riskier asset than bonds, it might last a bit longer or allow you to take out more each year. But then you risk losing a lot of principal in a market crash with comparatively little time left to make up the losses.

That amount of money might be plenty for most people. Not everyone has a burning desire to be wealthy. Some people just want a retirement where they don't have to worry about working so they can spend their days relaxing with family. But you may instead have to worry about having enough money just to keep living on what would be an average salary.

But what about Social Security benefits? Well, given the demographic reversion explained at the beginning of this Part, there is absolutely no guarantee that Social Security will remain the same system that it currently is. Social Security is already woefully underfunded, and the problem seems like it will only grow worse. Relying on Social Security benefits to fund a retirement beginning years from now is a dangerous proposition.

And while we're on the topic of government benefits, why not revisit the pension issue. Like the Social Security system, many states and localities have substantially underfunded pensions. For example, Illinois's pension deficit is over $130 billion as of 2020,[2] more than 15 percent of the state's entire GDP.

Even if a pension is currently "promised" by a state government, is it safe to assume that the government will not go back on its word out of necessity? The alternative appears to be bankruptcy. Governments throughout the country have made lofty promises with hardly the resources to fulfill them. It probably is best not to rely on those promises if you are aiming for a comfortable retirement.

Of course, there is always a chance that Social Security is overhauled to where it is properly funded. The same goes for pensions. But why not have insurance against the increasingly likely worst-case scenario? It makes a lot of sense to have control over your retirement, only leaving the government to provide a potential bonus to your nest egg rather than replacing the whole

[2] Reuters. (2019, December 4). *Illinois' Unfunded Pension Liability Rises to $137.3 Billion.* https://www.reuters.com/article/us-illinois-pensions/illinois-unfunded-pension-liability-rises-to-137-3-billion-idUSKBN1Y82ZP

thing. Sadly, especially with retirement money, less is not more.

With or without government-backed retirement benefits, there are a lot of potential costs to be prepared for in retirement. As we age, medical costs will undoubtedly increase. Whether that be drawn from savings to cover large bills or by paying for a comprehensive insurance plan, or even through taxes to fund a government-sponsored program, it will be expensive in any scenario. You may also have a larger extended family that you will want to spend time with and maybe even spoil. That can run up the tab, too.

And if you are not working at your career during your retirement days, what do you plan on doing? Are you going to stay at home all day doing nothing? Probably not. You will probably want a good amount of extra money to enjoy your days outside of your living room, maybe through shopping, eating at restaurants, and the other joys of capitalist America. But what if your budget is too tight because you did not save enough prior to retirement? Tough luck. Looks like you will not be able to afford much during your long, boring retirement.

In a weird twist of fate, you can also be penalized for living longer than you planned. Quite simply, you might run out of money in your retirement account because you happened to live to 92, rather than 85. This is a strangely unfortunate reality for many retirees, even those who might have saved up a respectable amount of money heading into retirement.

This is a big risk with having to live off of principal rather than interest or dividend income. By dipping into principal, you will dry up your investments much quicker than living off of any of their income. But stocks and bonds will only pay you so much income, and you would need a massive portfolio to have enough dividend stocks to live off of comfortably. Typically, a "good" dividend stock will have something like a 3 or 4 percent dividend yield. Dividend oriented funds typically pay about the same yield. To have a $50,000 salary from just dividend income, assuming a consistent 3.5 percent yield, you would need about $1.4 million in holdings. This is not to say that reaching that number is impossible, but get ready to work for quite a few more years to get there. And if you want to live off of more than that, you will dip into your principal, which will reduce your dividend income in turn.

Another consideration to make is that you may have to take mandatory withdrawals out of your 401(k) or IRA if your retirement holdings are parked there. This could ruin a dividend strategy, or at least make it significantly less tax efficient since you will have to buy and sell your holdings multiple times. Depending on your type of retirement account, this could be a taxable event and drastically reduce your earning power. Not to mention, that's just a hassle.

That said, the main takeaway here is that getting through retirement, even on a million-dollar nest egg of stocks on bonds, is not a guarantee of a smooth or prosperous retirement. And it might run dry years before you can afford it.

6. Control

Another particular problem with investing in stocks, bonds, and mutual funds is the inherent lack of control you have in the underlying assets. Stocks are sold on the open market and are subject to massive short run volatility. This can be a very big issue if you are trying to retire in the near future.

In our example above, you kept the same risk allocation the entire time. Your IRA was entirely stocks, which are higher risk than bonds. You would probably opt to switch more heavily into bonds by the time you neared retirement to ensure that a sudden market dip would not wipe away your retirement savings when you need them. This would lower your expected returns as well, meaning you would probably need to save more to make sure your savings last for more years.

In more extreme cases, the market can lose a huge portion of its value just over a few weeks. The Coronavirus pandemic I mentioned earlier is an unfortunately good example. The virus came out of seemingly nowhere and wreaked havoc on the stock market, which lost a good 20 percent of its value in just over a month in early 2020. Imagine being tied up in a mutual fund portfolio that lost that much of its value the year before you wanted to retire off of it. Looks like you will be working for a few more years to pick up the slack.

While stocks and bonds can offer handsome returns over the long run, they have a lot of short-term volatility that you really cannot do much about. Companies will make decisions that you do not want them to make, and this can affect their stock values. Irrational fears may plague the market and people will sell off very quickly. Government regulations might drastically change what companies can do or how investors can use the stock market. Simply put, there is a lot that is out of your control with stock investing, despite its benefits.

But you proclaim, "I don't care – I'll just turn it over to a financial planner and they'll take care of all of this for me and they'll be able to protect my money from shrinking." Even if your financial planner does beat the market, which is unlikely as it is, you are going to have to shell out some serious fees over many years. Some financial advisors charge fees as high as 1 or 2 percent of portfolio values, meaning that you will lose that amount of your portfolio each year *guaranteed* regardless of its actual performance. The price to surrender even more control for "convenience" is also expensive.

Regardless, there is no way to really avoid the volatility of the stock market unless you cash out of it entirely. Stocks can swing in any direction at seemingly any time. Trying to predict when a crash will happen is nearly impossible to do with any reliability. Or as Matthew McConaughey preached in *The Wolf of Wallstreet*:

> *"Number one rule of Wall Street: nobody, I don't care if you're Warren Buffet or if you're Jimmy Buffet, nobody knows if a stock is*

gonna go up, down, sideways or in f***ing circles, least of all stockbrokers."

Matthew's wisdom should not be taken lightly. His esteemed observation shows how your holdings will practically always be at risk of losing significant value very quickly. Losses might not be recovered for many years. And those years might be when you are trying to live off of your investments in retirement.

For those using tax advantaged accounts like IRAs and 401(k)s, or relying on the government through Social Security or publicly funded pensions, realize that the government can change the rules at any time. You might think that you are all set for retirement because of your sweet tax benefits, but then you will only be able to watch as the government drastically changes them a few years before you actually need to use the money. Similarly, as discussed above, massively underfunded pension systems are unsustainable and may see cuts despite initial promises by the government. With government sponsored programs and benefits, you are in the government's domain. That inherently comes with less control and is another avenue of risk. While I am not suggesting that an overhaul to the retirement system is likely or not, at least at the federal level, realize that you do not have control over the rules you are playing by.

In many cases, at least when you are educated in investing, the less control you have, the less safe your retirement. Real estate investing, on the other hand, is one way to increase your control in the underlying asset without losing a ton of the benefits of investing in the first place. That is the subject of the next third of the book, but I wanted to go over a very important requirement to investing successfully, first.

7. The Savings Hurdle

Before we go any further, it's important to understand the massive importance (and massive challenge) of being able to save your money.

Especially if you are new to retirement investing, you might have been shocked by the previous example where you were saving and investing $12,000 per year on a $40,000 salary. That's a big portion of your income, no doubt.

I'm not going to pretend like that's some walk in the park, especially if you have existing debts or otherwise unavoidable extra expenses.

But the fact of the matter is that you can do something about your budget to increase your savings rate. That might be through increasing your income through a side hustle or a job change, or by slashing your existing expenses. We'll go over some simple tips for increasing your savings in the following chapter, but I at least wanted to address this issue before we dive into the one property strategy.

If you struggle to save very much money each month, expect to take some extra time to build up a war chest. Even if it takes you many years to reach a specific savings goal, you'll be in a much better position than before.

To invest successfully, you are going to need to be able to save a lot of money. One of the biggest milestones in anyone's financial life is saving $100,000. Unfortunately, many do not ever achieve this incredibly impactful goal. That's certainly because it is a very difficult thing to do. For someone making a median salary, it will take years of discipline to get there.

One key to reaching a big savings goal is to divide it up into several smaller goals. If you are 23 and you want to save up $100,000 by the time you are 30, that gives you 7 years to work with. Now, work backwards. To reach $100,000 in 7 years, you'd need to save about $14,000 per year. That's about $1150 per month. Which is just under $275 per week. Now, rather than being intimidated by the large $100,000 figure, you can instead focus on developing an actionable plan to save $275 per week. If you have a breakeven budget each week, you'll have to figure out a way to "find" that money each week. The $275 can be broken down even further; you decide to cut $50 from your weekend fun budget, save $10 per week by getting a cheaper phone plan, utilize public transit rather than driving to work for another $40 in weekly savings, and earn an additional $175 per week by doing gig work. Now you're well on your way towards your savings goal! And all you had to do was find $275, not $100,000.

This is just a simple example. There are lots of ways to earn a little bit more money or spend a little bit less. Whatever your strategy, big goals are much more approachable when you break them down.

Whatever your actual salary is, find a way to automatically park money off to the side each month. Figure out what you're routinely spending money on and what areas in your budget are actually necessary. The only way to save is to be honest with yourself. What do you actually *need* versus what do you just *want*? You do not *need* an expensive car when you could buy a cheaper one (or forgo using a car altogether depending on where you live). You do not *need* to rent an apartment in your expensive downtown area when you could move 15 minutes away and save a few hundred bucks a month. You may certainly *want* those things, so it is up to you to prioritize how badly you actually want them instead of achieving your financial goals more quickly. Small sacrifices each month over a few years can add up and put you in a radically better position to advance financially.

When you can reach six figures in savings, you'll have some serious opportunities in front of you. As you'll see, $100,000 in cash can be used to buy many times that in real estate because of low-down-payment loans. A large, lump-sum investment can quickly transform your financial future.

The strategy proposed in the next chapter assumes that you are able to diligently save your money. It assumes that you can save your down payment so that you can get the ball rolling. This strategy, like practically all other investment strategies, will fail if you have to constantly pull money from it or otherwise burn through your savings.

As I mentioned, we'll return to savings strategies later on. Without further ado, let's get into the one property strategy.

II. The One Property Strategy

The one property strategy is exactly as it sounds. You buy one property, hold it, pay off the debt on it, and then reap the rewards.

But that sounds a lot like buying and holding stocks? Isn't real estate much harder to manage than just buying and holding stocks? Well, in one sense, that is correct. However, real estate has some unique advantages, mainly when it comes to long term debt options. When coupled with real estate's potential for producing income to be used towards debt payments, the one property strategy can unlock a simple path to lasting wealth.

This chapter is broken up into two parts: the first part explains the one property strategy in much greater detail, paying close attention to the numbers and what makes the strategy so powerful. The second part explains the mechanics of a deal and how you can execute the one property strategy yourself, even if you are brand new to real estate.

1. What's the One Property Strategy?

In this section, we'll go over the massive impact that the one property strategy can have on your retirement planning. But how does it work? What makes it great? We'll take a look at some amazing examples below.

The One Property Strategy Defined

Before beginning, you should have a target retirement number in mind. For consistency, let's say you want to have $4,000 in monthly passive income and a $1 million equity pool in retirement. For the purposes of this example, just like the last one with the stock portfolio, we will ignore inflation.

To use the one property strategy successfully, you should aim to purchase a $1 million property that you can rent out to cover any mortgage payments. In other words, when you are in retirement, your property's equity will be worth $1 million, sort of like your stock portfolio in the previous chapter's example.

Let's say you have been saving up some cash to buy your property. You know that you can get an owner-occupied mortgage loan that would cover 95 percent of the purchase price. This means you only need to bring about $50,000 in down payment money, plus the money to cover the $35,000 in estimated closing costs. You also want to make sure you have a solid reserve fund of $15,000 once you close. So, you need to save up $100,000 total before making the purchase.

$1 Million Real Estate Purchase	
Down Payment (5% of Price)	$50,000
Closing Costs	$35,000
Initial Reserves	$15,000
Total:	**$100,000**

You find a four-unit building listed for $1,000,000. It doesn't need any work, but only one of the units is occupied by a tenant. You will be moving into one of the units, so you will have to rent out the remaining two units as soon as possible after closing. The units are all the same layout, and would each earn about $2,000 in monthly rent.

Initial Projected Monthly Income	
Rent Per Unit (x3)	$2,000
Total:	**$6,000**

You get pre-approved for a $950,000 fixed-rate, 30-year mortgage loan at 4.25 percent interest. Your base loan payment will be about $4,600 each month. Because your loan to value is more than 80 percent, you will have to pay $400 in monthly mortgage insurance to the lender. Taxes and insurance come out to about $1,000 per month. Your fixed monthly expenses will be about $6,000. We will assume that the utilities for each unit are separately metered so each tenant will pay for his or her own utilities.

Initial Projected Monthly Expenses	
Mortgage Payment	$4,600
Private Mortgage Insurance	$400
Taxes & Insurance	$1,000
Total:	**$6,000**

So, while you live in this property, you will break even on the major expenses and debt service, minus any utilities that you pay for your own unit. Not a bad deal.

The plan is to move out of this property as soon as possible. Your loan requires you to live in at least one of the units during the first year, so you cannot rent it out to someone else during that time. But, once that first year passes, you will move out of the property and rent the unit that you were using. That would add an additional $2,000 in monthly rent.

Post-Move Out Projected Monthly Income	
Rent Per Unit (x4)	$2,000
Total:	**$8,000**

Once you move out, you are planning on turning it over to property management. You plan to set aside 25 percent of the rental income to cover your vacancy reserves, capital expenditures, and property management fees (all at around 8 percent of the monthly rent roll). This means that you would have no remaining cash flow once you move out, but you should be covered on all expenses and would be paying down your principal each month.

Post-Move Out Projected Monthly Expenses	
Mortgage Payment	$4,600
Private Mortgage Insurance	$400
Taxes & Insurance	$1,000
Vacancy & Capital Expenditures (17%)	$1,360
Property Management (8%)	$640
Total:	**$8,000**

You end up closing on the property, move into one unit, and immediately rent out the two vacant units. During this first year, you have $2,000 per month in lost rent, otherwise your tenants cover all other expenses. You move out of that unit after a year and rent out your former unit, just as you planned. You turn it over to a professional property manager and are now free to do whatever you want.

Where you go next is not very important; if you have the cash, you can buy a smaller property for your primary residence, with or without debt. Or you can rent an apartment. What you chose after this does not matter. What matters is that you have just acquired a break-even rental property worth $1 million that self-replenishes its reserves and is managed by someone else. And all it took was $100,000 in savings and 1 year of living in it.

At the end of year 10, your mortgage insurance payment will automatically drop off, so you will get $400 in additional monthly cash flow before the loan is paid off completely!

Year 10 Projected Monthly Income	
Rent Per Unit (x4)	$2,000
Total:	**$8,000**

Year 10 Projected Monthly Expenses	
Mortgage Payment	$4,600
~~Private Mortgage Insurance~~	~~$400~~
Taxes & Insurance	$1,000
Vacancy & Capital Expenditures (17%)	$1,360
Property Management (8%)	$640
Total:	**$7,600**

At the end of year 20, you will have about $440,000 of your mortgage loan left to pay off. At the end of year 30, you will pay off your mortgage and have a debt-free, $1,000,000 property that cash flows $6,000 per month ($8,000 in rent minus the capital expenditures, property management, and vacancy reserves expenses). That actually *overshoots* your retirement goal by $2,000 per month in income, plus you get the entire building's equity if you want to liquidate (or even re-leverage it with a cash-out refinance).

Your return on investment at the end of thirty years is also significantly higher than it would have been in the stock market. Between cash flow and principal paydown, you would have earned $1,026,800 in investment returns. That's over a 10-fold increase on your initial investment of $100,000, giving you an annualized return on investment of 34 percent!

Year	Cash Investment	Mortgage Balance	Equity	Cash Flow
0	$100,000.00	$950,000.00	$50,000.00	$0.00
1	$0.00	$933,984.27	$66,015.73	($24,000.00)
2	$0.00	$917,274.45	$82,725.55	$0.00
3	$0.00	$899,840.47	$100,159.53	$0.00
4	$0.00	$881,650.94	$118,349.06	$0.00
5	$0.00	$862,673.12	$137,326.88	$0.00
6	$0.00	$842,872.84	$157,127.16	$0.00
7	$0.00	$822,214.46	$177,785.54	$0.00
8	$0.00	$800,660.80	$199,339.20	$0.00
9	$0.00	$778,173.05	$221,826.95	$0.00
10	$0.00	$754,710.73	$245,289.27	$4,800.00
11	$0.00	$730,231.61	$269,768.39	$4,800.00
12	$0.00	$704,691.61	$295,308.39	$4,800.00
13	$0.00	$678,044.78	$321,955.22	$4,800.00
14	$0.00	$650,243.13	$349,756.87	$4,800.00
15	$0.00	$621,236.62	$378,763.38	$4,800.00
16	$0.00	$590,973.03	$409,026.97	$4,800.00
17	$0.00	$559,397.89	$440,602.11	$4,800.00
18	$0.00	$526,454.36	$473,545.64	$4,800.00
19	$0.00	$492,083.13	$507,916.87	$4,800.00
20	$0.00	$456,222.33	$543,777.67	$4,800.00
21	$0.00	$418,807.40	$581,192.60	$4,800.00
22	$0.00	$379,770.99	$620,229.01	$4,800.00
23	$0.00	$339,042.84	$660,957.16	$4,800.00
24	$0.00	$296,549.62	$703,450.38	$4,800.00
25	$0.00	$252,214.84	$747,785.16	$4,800.00
26	$0.00	$205,958.69	$794,041.31	$4,800.00
27	$0.00	$157,697.91	$842,302.09	$4,800.00
28	$0.00	$107,345.62	$892,654.38	$4,800.00
29	$0.00	$54,811.17	$945,188.83	$4,800.00
30	$0.00	$0.00	$1,000,000.00	$4,800.00

Total Investment:	$100,000.00
Total Cash Earnings:	$76,800.00
Total Principal Paydown:	$950,000.00
Total Return:	$1,026,800.00
Total ROI	1026.80%
Annualized ROI	34.23%

As a point of reference, a $100,000 lump sum investment invested in the stock market averaging a 7% annual growth rate for 30 years would net about a 23% annualized ROI, which is still good, but you'd have to continue exposing yourself to the short term volatility of the stock market the entire time. And you wouldn't have such a hefty revenue stream by the end.

But the example above assumes absolutely no appreciation in either rent or property value. Real estate tends to outpace inflation by a couple of percent each year on average, so your returns would likely be even higher. Here's the same example, this time with 1 percent annual appreciation in rent and property values:

Year	Cash Investment	Mortgage Balance	Equity	Cash Flow
0	$100,000.00	$950,000.00	$50,000.00	$0.00
1	$0.00	$933,984.27	$66,015.73	($24,000.00)
2	$0.00	$917,274.45	$92,725.55	$960.00
3	$0.00	$899,840.47	$120,259.53	$1,929.60
4	$0.00	$881,650.94	$148,650.06	$2,908.90
5	$0.00	$862,673.12	$177,930.89	$3,897.98
6	$0.00	$842,872.84	$208,137.21	$4,896.96
7	$0.00	$822,214.46	$239,305.69	$5,905.93
8	$0.00	$800,660.80	$271,474.56	$6,924.99
9	$0.00	$778,173.05	$304,683.66	$7,954.24
10	$0.00	$754,710.73	$338,974.55	$13,793.79
11	$0.00	$730,231.61	$374,390.52	$14,843.72
12	$0.00	$704,691.61	$410,976.73	$15,904.16
13	$0.00	$678,044.78	$448,780.25	$16,975.20
14	$0.00	$650,243.13	$487,850.15	$18,056.95
15	$0.00	$621,236.62	$528,237.59	$19,149.52
16	$0.00	$590,973.03	$569,995.92	$20,253.02
17	$0.00	$559,397.89	$613,180.75	$21,367.55
18	$0.00	$526,454.36	$657,850.07	$22,493.23
19	$0.00	$492,083.13	$704,064.35	$23,630.16
20	$0.00	$456,222.33	$751,886.63	$24,778.46
21	$0.00	$418,807.40	$801,382.64	$25,938.24
22	$0.00	$379,770.99	$852,620.95	$27,109.63
23	$0.00	$339,042.84	$905,673.02	$28,292.72
24	$0.00	$296,549.62	$960,613.40	$29,487.65
25	$0.00	$252,214.84	$1,017,519.81	$30,694.53
26	$0.00	$205,958.69	$1,076,473.30	$31,913.47
27	$0.00	$157,697.91	$1,137,558.40	$33,144.61
28	$0.00	$107,345.62	$1,200,863.26	$34,388.05
29	$0.00	$54,811.17	$1,266,479.80	$35,643.93
30	$0.00	$0.00	$1,334,503.88	$36,912.37

Total Investment:	$100,000.00
Total Cash Earnings:	$536,149.56
Total Appreciation:	$384,503.88
Total Principal Paydown:	$950,000.00
Total Return:	$1,870,653.44
Total ROI	1870.65%
Annualized ROI	62.36%

You will struggle to find an investment product that produces a 62 percent average annualized return without using debt. Even then, it might be difficult since real estate has access to some of the most favorable loan terms out there. And this is with a measly 1 percent in real annual appreciation. What about an investment with 2 percent appreciation per year on average, which is generally how real estate has historically performed?

Year	Cash Investment	Mortgage Balance	Equity	Cash Flow
0	$100,000.00	$950,000.00	$50,000.00	$0.00
1	$0.00	$933,984.27	$66,015.73	($24,000.00)
2	$0.00	$917,274.45	$102,725.55	$1,920.00
3	$0.00	$899,840.47	$140,559.53	$3,878.40
4	$0.00	$881,650.94	$179,557.06	$5,875.97
5	$0.00	$862,673.12	$219,759.04	$7,913.49
6	$0.00	$842,872.84	$261,207.96	$9,991.76
7	$0.00	$822,214.46	$303,947.96	$12,111.59
8	$0.00	$800,660.80	$348,024.87	$14,273.82
9	$0.00	$778,173.05	$393,486.34	$16,479.30
10	$0.00	$754,710.73	$440,381.84	$23,528.89
11	$0.00	$730,231.61	$488,762.81	$25,823.46
12	$0.00	$704,691.61	$538,682.69	$28,163.93
13	$0.00	$678,044.78	$590,197.02	$30,551.21
14	$0.00	$650,243.13	$643,363.50	$32,986.24
15	$0.00	$621,236.62	$698,242.14	$35,469.96
16	$0.00	$590,973.03	$754,895.30	$38,003.36
17	$0.00	$559,397.89	$813,387.81	$40,587.43
18	$0.00	$526,454.36	$873,787.06	$43,223.18
19	$0.00	$492,083.13	$936,163.12	$45,911.64
20	$0.00	$456,222.33	$1,000,588.85	$48,653.87
21	$0.00	$418,807.40	$1,067,140.00	$51,450.95
22	$0.00	$379,770.99	$1,135,895.35	$54,303.97
23	$0.00	$339,042.84	$1,206,936.83	$57,214.05
24	$0.00	$296,549.62	$1,280,349.65	$60,182.33
25	$0.00	$252,214.84	$1,356,222.41	$63,209.98
26	$0.00	$205,958.69	$1,434,647.30	$66,298.18
27	$0.00	$157,697.91	$1,515,720.20	$69,448.14
28	$0.00	$107,345.62	$1,599,540.86	$72,661.10
29	$0.00	$54,811.17	$1,686,213.04	$75,938.32
30	$0.00	$0.00	$1,775,844.69	$79,281.09

Total Investment:	**$100,000.00**
Total Cash Earnings:	$1,091,335.61
Total Appreciation:	$825,844.69
Total Principal Paydown:	$950,000.00
Total Return:	**$2,867,180.30**
Total ROI	2867.18%
Annualized ROI	95.57%

I think the message is clear by now. Even an *average* deal that appreciates just a little bit each year can produce astounding returns.

Compare this to stocks. To have $6,000 in monthly passive income with dividend stocks, in addition to $1 million in *extra* equity with your other holdings, you would need to have about $2.7 million in total stock holdings. Real estate's income producing power is tremendous. And real estate debt is incredibly accessible and relatively cheap.

But how does debt help here? What exactly does it do to make this strategy produce such high returns? Let's master the magic of debt now.

The Magic of Debt

Perhaps the most misunderstood concept in the personal finance realm, debt is something that should not be ignored.

Debt has helped to create many millionaires and billionaires, if not most of them. It has also put at least as many people on the path to bankruptcy. The key to the former's success is specifically using *good debt* to finance their projects. The latter took out *bad debt* which did not produce them something in return. Not all debt is bad. Not all debt is good. Understanding the difference between good debt and bad debt is a key to unlocking your true potential for building wealth.

Bad debt is debt that will not help you to build wealth or generate income. Bad debt does not provide you enough in return. A common example of bad debt is most credit card debt. Too often, people will use a credit card to buy something that they cannot otherwise afford and are then stuck paying 20 percent in interest until they pay it off, which can take years for some. They might rack up debt to finance expensive vacations, eat at fancy restaurants, or purchase other luxuries.

The problem with financing those items (especially at such high interest rates) is that they will not produce anything to help pay the debt back. That is, financing a vacation won't produce any new income. Instead, the person will have to pull from other assets to pay down the debt for a net loss. Bad debt happens when people ignore this fundamental question: *would it make more sense to buy this with cash?*

If the answer to that question is yes, taking out debt is not a good idea. It would be best to wait until you actually have the money to buy that item. Otherwise, it will only be driving you backwards. If you fall too far behind, you might suffer truly terrible financial consequences. If the answer is no, then using debt might make sense.

Good debt is the kind of debt that can help you. Good debt is often called "leverage." For example, if you can finance a used car (that you actually need for your job, let's say) at 4 percent interest and then take the money that you would have used to buy the car in cash and invest it in the stock market to make a 7 percent return, that debt is good debt. Your money is being used more productively elsewhere while someone else's money is used to buy the thing that you want.

The same concept applies to real estate. One of the best examples of good debt is a real estate investor financing the purchase of a multifamily property. Let's say the complex is worth $1,000,000. The investor could try to buy it with all cash. That person would need to fork over the entire lump sum of $1,000,000. That doesn't seem too practical. Alternatively, the investor can take out a $750,000 mortgage at 5% interest and only have to put up $250,000 in cash.

If the expected annual return on the property is 10 percent thanks to the rental income, taking out the mortgage at only 5 percent does not make the deal unprofitable. Instead, it allows the investor to use his or her remaining cash elsewhere. Meanwhile, the property will bring in rental income that will be used to pay down the mortgage. The investor will build equity as the mortgage is consistently paid down. The investor will also take home some cash flow each month after paying off expenses. Once the property is paid off, all of the income that would have gone to mortgage payments will become free cash flow!

That said, you can have too much good debt. Let's say you use debt to buy a rental property. You don't have the cash to cover the down payment, but you are able to get another loan to cover the down payment. In this case, you are financing 100% of the property. Even though it's a lot of debt, it's all going to an income producing asset, so it's good, right?

Perhaps. But what happens if rents drop in the area and the rental income can't cover all of that debt? And maybe you face a slight pay cut at your job. You now cannot afford to pay for the property because you over-leveraged yourself. There's too much "good" debt and not enough income being produced to pay for it. In that way, the good debt becomes bad.

Leverage and real estate are part of a delicate balancing act. Debt is a weapon; it must be used responsibly to avoid unnecessary injury.

Over-leveraging is a common problem for investors. When times are good, investors often take out as much debt as they possibly can. When times are bad, those investors who are over-leveraged crumble. Warren Buffett, for example, makes sure to always keep a substantial pile of cash for his company to avoid a potential liquidity crisis. Incomes often decrease in hard times while fixed debt payments stay the same. If you do not have an emergency fund set up to cover yourself in hard times, you potentially expose yourself to the terrible pain of over-leveraging. Borrow with caution! All of that said, debt used to buy a (preferably) cash flowing property is the good debt that can pave your way towards retirement.

Assuming you are adequately protected by some cash reserves, you can create much greater returns by using good debt. However, this is not without risk. Generally, the more good debt you use, the higher your potential reward but the higher your risk. Conversely, the less debt you use, the lower your potential reward but the lower your risk.

Some debt might start off as good debt but transforms into bad debt because of some other factor. For example, if someone gets a variable rate mortgage that starts off at 2 percent interest, but years later climbs to 8 percent and causes the property to produce negative cash flow, debt that was once good is now bad. The "goodness" of debt is relative. Thankfully, the real estate industry makes it fairly easy to secure long-term, fixed-rate debt, eliminating interest rate risk.

There is no right answer for how much risk you should take. Some people are far more comfortable with a lot of risk. Others would rather keep everything in cash and avoid as much risk as possible. But, without some debt, it is unlikely you are going to avoid the scenario presented in the first chapter: slow, grueling investing over 30 years at your job that you may or may not like, taking away time (and money) from all of the other things that you want to do.

Real estate is one of the most powerful investment vehicles that encourages using debt. While people might raise an eyebrow to you buying stocks on margin, they probably won't think much of you using debt on real estate. After all, the mortgage and mortgage-backed-securities market is one of the biggest sectors in the financial world. Homeowners and investors are no strangers to debt. Maybe you are still skeptical; let's take a detailed look at what debt can do to your return on investment.

Let's say you have $100,000 in cash that you would like to invest. You find a piece of real estate that would make a nice rental property, and you get it under contract for a $100,000 sales price. You can decide to buy the property in all cash. You pour all of your available cash into it, so you do not have any debt on the property. After a year, the property rises in value by $10,000. You also bring in $5,000 in rental cash flow. If you sell the property, you will walk away with a solid 15% return. Here's a recap:

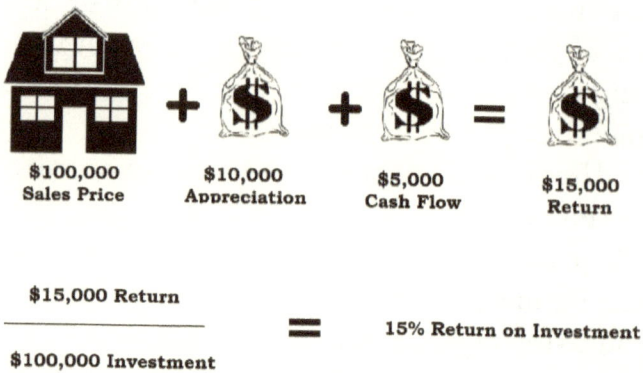

$100,000
Sales Price

$10,000
Appreciation

$5,000
Cash Flow

$15,000
Return

$$\frac{\$15,000 \text{ Return}}{\$100,000 \text{ Investment}} = 15\% \text{ Return on Investment}$$

Take that same $100,000 property, but now assume you used an $80,000 mortgage to buy it. You used $20,000 in cash as your down payment. Let's assume that the property doesn't even cash flow; all the rent is used to pay the mortgage and expenses and there is nothing left over. Now when the property appreciates by $10,000, even with no cash flow, you just made a 50% return. You also still have $80,000 of your cash left over since you only invested $20,000. It would look something like this:

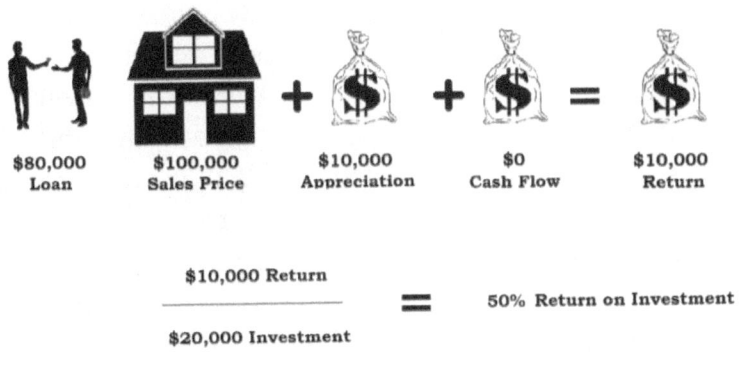

$80,000 Loan $100,000 Sales Price $10,000 Appreciation $0 Cash Flow $10,000 Return

$$\frac{\$10,000 \text{ Return}}{\$20,000 \text{ Investment}} = 50\% \text{ Return on Investment}$$

On top of that, with a leveraged property, the rent coming in will be used to pay down the mortgage balance over time. And because the loan is not your money, you are practically getting something out of nothing. You have purchased the revenue stream (the property) using a loan, and the revenue stream is used to pay down the loan. You keep the revenue stream once the loan is paid off. And you only have to pay a fraction of the cost up front.

As long as the property is well positioned and brings in enough rent to cover the mortgage and maintain reserves, you should be in great shape for the long run. That property you bought will pay itself off in time and you will have a significant asset to retire off of.

Every dollar you have could theoretically be used to buy $4 or $5 in real estate, if not more. That is, you can multiply your purchasing power with debt. Then, when your debt is paid off, well, that's a lot of real estate. If you are looking to build wealth quickly, debt is likely going to be a very important tool. Cash is comparatively slow.

When you have no debt, you will not have to worry about paying other folks first if things go south. At the same time, without using debt, you will likely forgo many opportunities that could help you build wealth rapidly and succeed financially.

Technically, you can use the one property strategy without any debt, but then you would have to make all of the cash to buy the property in advance. For a property that can adequately fund a retirement, you would probably be looking at the same $1 million lump sum that you would earn by slowly investing in stocks during that whole time. Long-term, fixed-interest debt is what makes this strategy so powerful.

An Increasing Revenue Stream

Let's take a moment to revisit some of the things that make the one property strategy effective. One of real estate's most powerful tools is its income producing potential. With the one property strategy, you would typically start out with high debt and low cash flow. But, as rent appreciates, your cash flow stream will also grow since your debt costs should be fixed. If you have private mortgage insurance, you will get another nice boost to cash flow once you reach 78 percent equity on the original loan since that is typically when PMI drops off.

Once the loan is paid off, cash flow will increase immediately. While your flexibility will grow as you build more equity in the property, you will have the ultimate flexibility via cash flow once the loan is gone. As Anakin Skywalker once said, "This is where the fun begins."

Let's take a look at the example with absolutely no real appreciation. This property and its rent only follow inflation and produce no additional real return. I have included years 30

through 45 to show what you would be making
during retirement as well.

Year	Cash Investment	Mortgage Balance	Equity	Cash Flow
0	$100,000.00	$950,000.00	$50,000.00	$0.00
1	$0.00	$933,984.27	$66,015.73	($24,000.00)
2	$0.00	$917,274.45	$82,725.55	$0.00
3	$0.00	$899,840.47	$100,159.53	$0.00
4	$0.00	$881,650.94	$118,349.06	$0.00
5	$0.00	$862,673.12	$137,326.88	$0.00
6	$0.00	$842,872.84	$157,127.16	$0.00
7	$0.00	$822,214.46	$177,785.54	$0.00
8	$0.00	$800,660.80	$199,339.20	$0.00
9	$0.00	$778,173.05	$221,826.95	$0.00
10	$0.00	$754,710.73	$245,289.27	$4,800.00
11	$0.00	$730,231.61	$269,768.39	$4,800.00
12	$0.00	$704,691.61	$295,308.39	$4,800.00
13	$0.00	$678,044.78	$321,955.22	$4,800.00
14	$0.00	$650,243.13	$349,756.87	$4,800.00
15	$0.00	$621,236.62	$378,763.38	$4,800.00
16	$0.00	$590,973.03	$409,026.97	$4,800.00
17	$0.00	$559,397.89	$440,602.11	$4,800.00
18	$0.00	$526,454.36	$473,545.64	$4,800.00
19	$0.00	$492,083.13	$507,916.87	$4,800.00
20	$0.00	$456,222.33	$543,777.67	$4,800.00
21	$0.00	$418,807.40	$581,192.60	$4,800.00
22	$0.00	$379,770.99	$620,229.01	$4,800.00
23	$0.00	$339,042.84	$660,957.16	$4,800.00
24	$0.00	$296,549.62	$703,450.38	$4,800.00
25	$0.00	$252,214.84	$747,785.16	$4,800.00
26	$0.00	$205,958.69	$794,041.31	$4,800.00
27	$0.00	$157,697.91	$842,302.09	$4,800.00
28	$0.00	$107,345.62	$892,654.38	$4,800.00
29	$0.00	$54,811.17	$945,188.83	$4,800.00
30	$0.00	$0.00	$1,000,000.00	$4,800.00
31	$0.00	$0.00	$1,000,000.00	$64,800.00
32	$0.00	$0.00	$1,000,000.00	$64,800.00
33	$0.00	$0.00	$1,000,000.00	$64,800.00
34	$0.00	$0.00	$1,000,000.00	$64,800.00
35	$0.00	$0.00	$1,000,000.00	$64,800.00
36	$0.00	$0.00	$1,000,000.00	$64,800.00
37	$0.00	$0.00	$1,000,000.00	$64,800.00
38	$0.00	$0.00	$1,000,000.00	$64,800.00
39	$0.00	$0.00	$1,000,000.00	$64,800.00
40	$0.00	$0.00	$1,000,000.00	$64,800.00
41	$0.00	$0.00	$1,000,000.00	$64,800.00
42	$0.00	$0.00	$1,000,000.00	$64,800.00
43	$0.00	$0.00	$1,000,000.00	$64,800.00
44	$0.00	$0.00	$1,000,000.00	$64,800.00
45	$0.00	$0.00	$1,000,000.00	$64,800.00

Notice how you do get some extra cash flow once your private mortgage insurance drops off in year ten. Once your loan is paid off, your cash flow is freed up dramatically.

Even when you are not cash flowing handsomely, you are still constantly building net worth by paying down the loan balance. Here's a graph of your net worth gains each year:

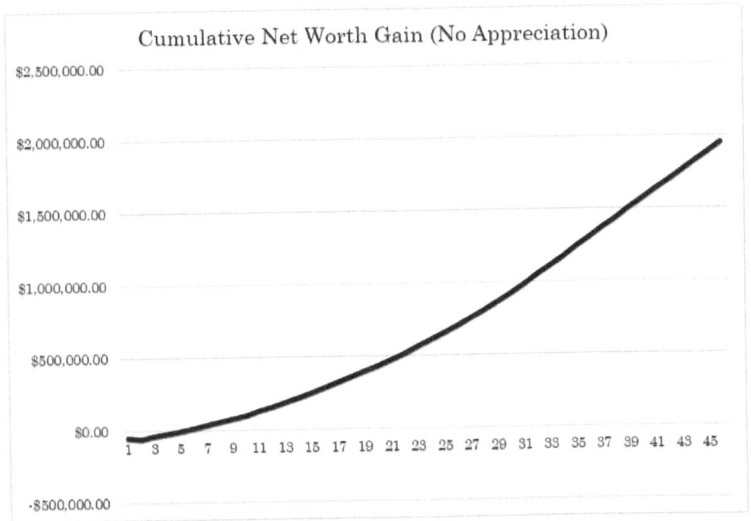

This assumes that all of your cash flow is kept or invested into something that will not lose its value. But the point is clear: your net worth growth accelerates over the life of the loan and then peaks at retirement (when the loan is paid off). Even if you end up spending all of your cash flow on other things, you still end up with a large amount of equity and a stable income stream.

What about the example we explored at the beginning of this chapter with 2 percent real appreciation each year? Here's what that would look like:

Year	Cash Investment	Mortgage Balance	Equity	Cash Flow
0	$100,000.00	$950,000.00	$50,000.00	$0.00
1	$0.00	$933,984.27	$66,015.73	($24,000.00)
2	$0.00	$917,274.45	$102,725.55	$1,920.00
3	$0.00	$899,840.47	$140,559.53	$3,878.40
4	$0.00	$881,650.94	$179,557.06	$5,875.97
5	$0.00	$862,673.12	$219,759.04	$7,913.49
6	$0.00	$842,872.84	$261,207.96	$9,991.76
7	$0.00	$822,214.46	$303,947.96	$12,111.59
8	$0.00	$800,660.80	$348,024.87	$14,273.82
9	$0.00	$778,173.05	$393,486.34	$16,479.30
10	$0.00	$754,710.73	$440,381.84	$23,528.89
11	$0.00	$730,231.61	$488,762.81	$25,823.46
12	$0.00	$704,691.61	$538,682.69	$28,163.93
13	$0.00	$678,044.78	$590,197.02	$30,551.21
14	$0.00	$650,243.13	$643,363.50	$32,986.24
15	$0.00	$621,236.62	$698,242.14	$35,469.96
16	$0.00	$590,973.03	$754,895.30	$38,003.36
17	$0.00	$559,397.89	$813,387.81	$40,587.43
18	$0.00	$526,454.36	$873,787.06	$43,223.18
19	$0.00	$492,083.13	$936,163.12	$45,911.64
20	$0.00	$456,222.33	$1,000,588.85	$48,653.87
21	$0.00	$418,807.40	$1,067,140.00	$51,450.95
22	$0.00	$379,770.99	$1,135,895.35	$54,303.97
23	$0.00	$339,042.84	$1,206,936.83	$57,214.05
24	$0.00	$296,549.62	$1,280,349.65	$60,182.33
25	$0.00	$252,214.84	$1,356,222.41	$63,209.98
26	$0.00	$205,958.69	$1,434,647.30	$66,298.18
27	$0.00	$157,697.91	$1,515,720.20	$69,448.14
28	$0.00	$107,345.62	$1,599,540.86	$72,661.10
29	$0.00	$54,811.17	$1,686,213.04	$75,938.32
30	$0.00	$0.00	$1,775,844.69	$79,281.09
31	$0.00	$0.00	$1,811,361.58	$142,690.71
32	$0.00	$0.00	$1,847,588.82	$146,168.53
33	$0.00	$0.00	$1,884,540.59	$149,715.90
34	$0.00	$0.00	$1,922,231.40	$153,334.21
35	$0.00	$0.00	$1,960,676.03	$157,024.90
36	$0.00	$0.00	$1,999,889.55	$160,789.40
37	$0.00	$0.00	$2,039,887.34	$164,629.18
38	$0.00	$0.00	$2,080,685.09	$168,545.77
39	$0.00	$0.00	$2,122,298.79	$172,540.68
40	$0.00	$0.00	$2,164,744.77	$176,615.50
41	$0.00	$0.00	$2,208,039.66	$180,771.81
42	$0.00	$0.00	$2,252,200.46	$185,011.24
43	$0.00	$0.00	$2,297,244.47	$189,335.47
44	$0.00	$0.00	$2,343,189.36	$193,746.18
45	$0.00	$0.00	$2,390,053.14	$198,245.10

That's a pretty comfortable retirement, if I do say so myself. You make six figures *and* have a multimillion-dollar equity moat. If, for some reason, you needed more cash during retirement, you could re-leverage that large amount of equity with a line of credit or an equity loan. In other words, you have a strong revenue stream with a built-in safety net of equity. You could always sell the property in a pinch and move it into a "safer" asset like bonds.

But selling would eliminate this ever-increasing cash flow stream. Note the sudden jump in cash flow at the end of year 30, the year you finish paying off your loan. This is completely separate from your property's equity:

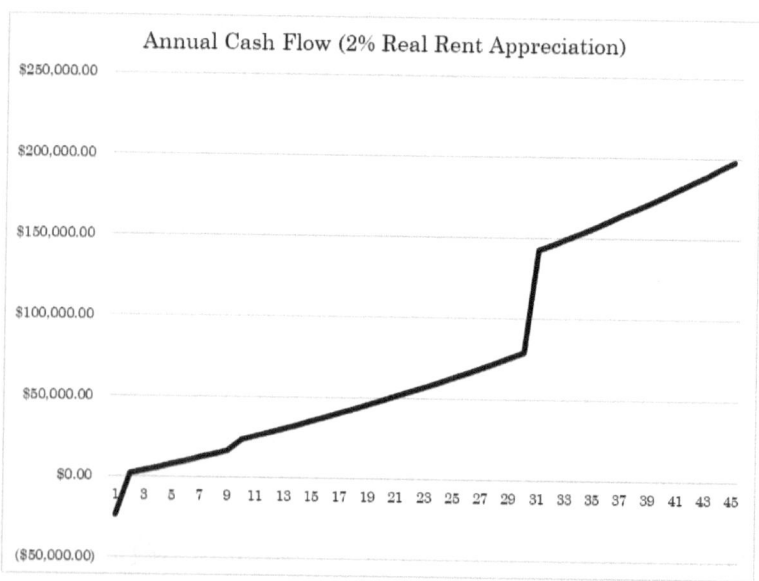

You can look at this chart as your salary, only that this "salary" is all derived from the property's rental income. And this is your salary after a single, lump sum investment at the very beginning.

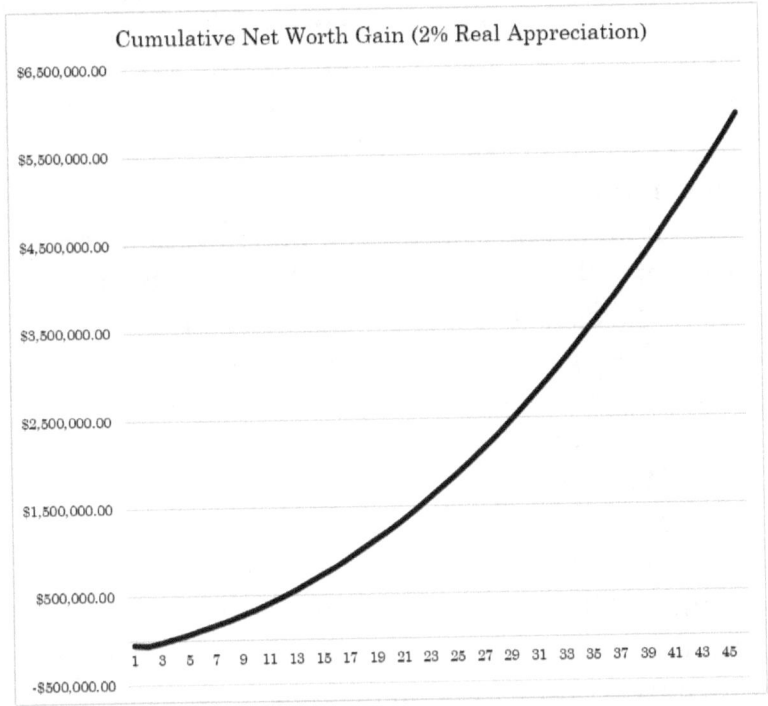

And your net worth will grow exponentially, too. Any rent and equity appreciation will only accelerate your growth even more.

Simply put, the one property strategy thrives in the final third of its life. That's when the property's complete income potential is realized. Debt payments are shaved off, maximum equity and cash flow are achieved.

In looking at all of the previous examples, note how appreciation was not critical. Appreciation is certainly a nice bonus, but, in each situation, you had sufficient income to retire off of. This was regardless of whether there was any appreciation.

Real estate typically follows inflation at the very least. Rent typically does the same. So, the vast majority of the time, real estate should work as a hedge against inflation. However, this is not unique from stocks and many other assets, which also typically rise, minimally, with inflation.

What is critical with the one property strategy is that *other peoples' money* (i.e. the bank's loan) is being paid for by *other people* (your tenants). All of this creates a magical situation where you can create a retirement nest egg after only putting up a fraction of the cash at the beginning.

Most importantly, the one property strategy creates options. That is the subject of the third and final part of this book, which will explain the different financial avenues and opportunities the one property strategy can unlock. But, before we get to that, let's go over how to actually carry out the one property strategy from beginning to end.

2. How to Execute the One Property Strategy

Now that you understand what makes the one property strategy so powerful, how do you go about doing it? Buying real estate has many more steps than buying stocks. And you really have to do your due diligence before you close a deal. That's not always the case with stocks; but, with real estate, going into a deal blind can have enormous consequences.

We'll go through all of the steps for carrying out a deal in great detail below, but here they are for your reference:

1. Build your real estate buying team
2. Figure out what type of mortgage you want to use
3. Save up for your down payment
4. Get approved for a mortgage
5. Search for your property
6. Rent out the property

7. Maintain the property

Let's start with one of the most important steps – building your team.

Building Your Real Estate Team

Real estate is a true team game. You will never be able to buy a property completely by yourself, even if you buy in all cash. Well, theoretically, if you buy a house entirely in cash without an agent, represent yourself as a licensed attorney, skip inspection, and are an insurance agent, you might be able to pull it off. You would almost certainly make a significant mistake, unfortunately, unless the other side was willing to push closing a couple of months back to give you extra time to sort through the issues. You need a team to buy real estate!

If you are just starting out, you probably have a small network. This can be an excuse for a lot of people who say they want to invest to keep putting it off. "Well, I don't know anyone." Yeah? Go meet some people! Thankfully, the internet has made bringing people together much easier, and the COVID-19 era has shown how useful video conferencing can be for convenient meet ups.

Besides that, it is very likely that someone in your family or close friend group knows someone (or is someone!) who works or invests in real estate. Do not pretend like you have to attend large, corporate networking events to find someone reliable. That is only one way to do things.

Building your network is useful beyond real estate. The more people you know, the wider your network and the more people who would be willing to trust you or help you out. If you have zero trusted contacts who would be willing to introduce you to others, you should do everything you can to show people that you can provide value in some way. Sometimes that value might just be giving someone your undivided attention. The ability to tag along on your future deal(s) is something that you can offer as well.

Who should be on your team? As a buyer, you definitely should utilize an agent familiar with the area. You will need a trustworthy lender as well. You'll also need a real estate attorney and a licensed home inspector. You will also need an insurance agent or someone who can supply you with a homeowner's policy. If the house happens to need some repairs or updating, you will potentially need contractors like electricians, plumbers, painters, or carpenters, among others. And, unless you chose to self-manage, you will need a property manager. We will look at each member of your team in detail below.

Agent

On the buying side, a real estate agent simply helps you shop for properties. Agents come at all different skill levels, and are generally very geographically specialized. This means that someone based in Chicago would probably not be too knowledgeable (or helpful) about Carbondale real estate (which is over 300 miles south of Chicago, for those of you not from the great state of Illinois). Make sure that your agent is licensed in the state that you are looking in, as license requirements vary from state to state.[3]

Agents gain access to a Multiple Listing Service (MLS) that they can use to search for listed properties. Many states require an agent to be present to enter a listed property. Everyday buyers do not get access to the MLS, although they can search for most listed deals through larger online providers (like Zillow or Redfin among many others) for free.

---

[3] If you need a real estate agent in the Chicagoland area, feel free to reach out at www.jackduffleyagent.com!

An agent makes his or her commission from the listing seller's listing fee. When people put their properties on the market using an agent (as most people do) their listing agent gets a percentage of the sales price as a commission. If the listing agent finds a buyer for the seller, the listing agent keeps the entire commission. However, when a buyer's agent brings a buyer to another agent's listing, that listing agent and the buyer's agent generally split the commission fifty-fifty. The important note here is that the seller is paying the same amount of commission either way, and the buyer is not paying anything to use the buyer's agent.

In short, it is advantageous to use an agent when you're shopping for a property. They do not cost you anything, since the seller will pay their commission based on their pre-determined listing fee, and they can give you a very useful perspective on the local area. Perhaps more importantly, they can help connect you with other buyers, sellers, and the eventual other members of your team should you not have them picked out already.

Good agents can be tough to find. It is relatively easy to become an agent, but it takes a lot of hard work to be a good one. Consider reaching out to local brokerages and trying to find an agent who is very familiar with the local market, specifically in the neighborhood(s) that you are looking in. An agent who invests in the area is an added bonus.

That said, your agent, unless licensed to practice law, should not act as your attorney. Agents are not allowed to give legal advice or draft legal documents. They can obviously speak to their personal experience, but do check over riskier legal questions with your attorney should any arise. Your agent should act as a useful guide but should not supersede your attorney.

Some investors end up getting their real estate license so that they can browse the MLS and book showings themselves. This can be a good idea for a few reasons: not only will you have to complete a rather lengthy course on real estate which can help you to get comfortable with the process, you can have greater flexibility as an investor and access to the most extensive real estate listing information possible. Furthermore, it can be a great potential career path for those willing to put in the time and the effort. Getting your license is certainly not necessary, however. Most investors do great without one. It is a matter of personal preference only.

When you search for your agent, if he or she has other priorities that might hinder your ability to go for deals, consider finding a new one. That goes for any team member; if there is someone who fits into your plans better, do what you can to move them onto your team! Your agent is one of your main contacts throughout the deal, especially during the early stages, so make sure that you pick the right fit so the whole process gets off on the right foot!

Lender

Your lender is arguably your most important team member (unless you are buying with all cash!). Closing takes as long as it does for most deals because the lender needs the most time to make sure that you and the property are worth the risk to them.

How do you find a lender? Simply put, you have to ask around. There are tons of lenders out there, some institutional, some not. If this is your first deal and your credit is rather new (but clean and strong!) you should probably opt to use a traditional lender rather than someone offering a different type of creative financing.

By traditional lenders, I mean banks and credit unions. These businesses deal with mortgages all the time; they are a significant aspect, and sometimes the vast majority, of their respective businesses. Ideally, you should use a lender with plenty of experience to avoid unnecessary hiccups and added uncertainty. If that lender is a larger bank, experience shouldn't really be an issue. Whichever lender you pick, make sure to do your homework!

Some banks, like the big national chains, may offer very strong rates but will have stricter standards, especially thanks to what happened leading up to the 2008 crash when everyone and their dog were able to take on very risky mortgages. Banks have much stricter, regulated standards to try and avoid the catastrophe that was the recession. Smaller lenders might have a bit more flexibility in who they can lend to, generally, but they too are subject to rigid federal standards, especially when they are using FHA, VA, or other government insured loans.

Regional lenders may be more comfortable lending on certain properties in your area. They may also be able to answer more questions about a specific type of strategy relevant to your neighborhood. However, local branches of huge banks might also have plenty of area specialists, so it is not to say that only regional banks offer this.

It's important to shop around to see who has a good reputation in the area you are trying to invest in! In the long run, establishing a strong relationship with one or a few lenders can ensure that you will have access to financing should you want to refinance or move beyond this first property.

Before you actually begin searching, you should know what kind of financing that you are looking for. If you're taking advantage of one of the government-sponsored, owner-occupied loans, let your lender know right away. There are a lot of different types of loans that you can get. See what your specific lender offers and on what terms. Don't worry, we'll go over the different types of real estate loans shortly.

It is important to watch out for hidden fees, especially if you have not used a particular lender in the past. By asking multiple lenders about their rates and fees, you will be able to determine whether or not the lender you are planning on using is giving you competitive rates and is charging reasonable fees. If not, it is very likely time to move on to someone else. Just be careful!

When choosing a lender, you should be evaluating them just as you would any other member of your team. Are the people from that bank or lending team honest? Are they putting things in plain English for you or at least explaining anything that you do not understand? Are they telling you that you cannot do something even though other lenders say you can? If your lender does not pass the "smell test," it is probably best to avoid them.

We'll talk about actually getting approved for a mortgage in a later section.

Attorney

Your attorney functions as your chief informant. He or she should typically be the first to let you know about an issue with title, property taxes, or some other issue with the property. A good attorney can also be a great help in answering the questions you might have about the types of legal risk that you might be exposing yourself to with a deal.

There are two types of attorneys you should consider for any real estate deal: a *real estate* attorney or a commercial *real estate* attorney. Both types are specialized for real estate transactions. Avoid using a general practitioner or a firm that is not accustomed to doing real estate transactions. A traditional real estate attorney will be able to help you with your residential deals from inception to closing. A commercial real estate attorney, if applicable, will be one that can help create your entity structure or in navigating more complex deals (like non-residential deals). Depending on how you purchase your deal, a commercial real estate attorney can help you to setup an entity structure to best protect yourself from personal liability that may arise out of running rental properties. In the event that you are using owner-occupied financing, you likely will have to purchase the property in your name, though you might explore moving the property into an entity later on. Definitely review this issue with your attorney.

A commercial real estate attorney, as opposed to a typical residential real estate attorney, might be overkill for a smaller, residential deal bought in your own name. And "smaller" is relative; commercial real estate attorneys often deal with transactions well into the millions and up. Commercial real estate attorneys are typically more expensive; they are specialized to work on more complex deals than a small single or multi-family building purchase. However, once entities are involved, or the size of the deal becomes significantly larger, it might make more sense to consult a commercial real estate attorney instead of a residential one. Otherwise, you likely will be totally fine using a solid residential real estate attorney on your deal.

Whichever type of attorney you use, again, he or she should be specialized in real estate transactions. An attorney who drafted your will probably is not the best option for your real estate deal, and neither is an attorney who normally helps you get out of traffic tickets. Errors by your attorney during the buying stage can carry massive, long-term consequences. You want someone who knows what he or she is doing in the area of real estate specifically.

Once you have found that person, your attorney should be able to help you with any questions regarding your prospective deal. That said, the attorney's role tends to be on the backend; attorneys deal with the title company, lender, agent, the other side's attorney, and, if applicable, the homeowners association in collecting everything necessary for closing. Attorneys also play a key role in many states in adjusting sales contracts during the first few days after getting something under contract. This is called the "attorney review period" in those states that have one. Either way, if there are any title issues or other legal issues, your attorney should bring them to your attention.

At closing, your attorney will be present and will help walk you through all of the mortgage and title documents. If you are doing a remote closing, which is becoming increasingly common, you may be able to go through all of those documents and sign them without being physically present on closing day. Regardless, your attorney should be the one who points out any discrepancies and clears up any questions before the end of closing.

Some states actually do not require attorneys to close a real estate deal. Even if you don't have to use one, you should strongly consider hiring one. It's an extra line of defense for you and probably is worth the extra few hundred bucks.

If you don't use an attorney, be sure to find a solid title company to work with depending on whether the buyer or seller selects the title company. Each state is a little different. But the title company and the attorney in a deal usually keep tabs on each other and share a lot of information to make sure that the title on a property is clean and that everything is in line prior to closing.

Regardless, if you need a real estate attorney, consider asking your agent or someone else that you know if they've had a good experience with one. One of the best and really easiest ways to add a quality member to your team is to ask around as opposed to diving into a long google search and guessing who is good. Just ask someone you trust for an introduction!

Inspector

No matter what type of property or its size, it is always a good bet to use a property inspector. Especially if this is your first deal, you absolutely should use one. Inspectors typically must go through rigorous licensing and need to know how to spot otherwise hard-to-find problems in a piece of real estate.

Once you have a property under contract, if not beforehand, you should have your inspector take a look at it as soon as possible. As I mentioned earlier, there is often an attorney review period once something is under contract. During this time, your inspector should take a look at the building and point out anything that might be out of line. The inspector will send over a written report with a recap of his or her findings. You can forward the report and bring up the property's problems with your attorney.

Not only does this put a second set of very well-trained eyes on the property, basically anything that you did not realize about the property that the inspector points out can be used as cause to back out of the contract (unless your contract unconventionally says otherwise – make sure to double check with your attorney!). Even better, your attorney can raise the issues from the inspector's report to try and get some credits at closing.

A credit at closing is money that the other side will give to you at the end of the deal. It cancels out part if not all of your closing expenses. In many ways, a credit is like a coupon given to you by the other side.

Why would another side give credits at closing? Sometimes, inspection may reveal new problems that both sides might have been unaware of when they negotiated the initial buying price. Rather than start over with a brand-new contract, the selling side can agree to just throw in a credit at closing for the buying side to keep them along for the deal. A buyer has the leverage from being able to back out of the deal if the seller doesn't agree. Often, credits can be negotiated at the beginning of a contract to cover many aspects of closing costs depending on the seller's motivations and the state of the property. They are simply an added level of negotiable flexibility.

Insurance

If you have already bought insurance for other items in the past, you should probably start by reaching out to your insurance agent to ask for homeowner's insurance policies. If you do not have an insurance agent, or you dislike your current one, find a new one. An agent will be able to walk you through your policy options. Depending on the type of property you are buying, you should adjust your liability coverage accordingly.

A lot of insurance companies offer bundling for different types of policies (like home and automobile insurance). You should consider taking advantage of these sorts of discount programs if it makes sense to use a provider that you happen to already be using for another type of insurance.

After you buy the property and get your initial policy, be sure to avoid becoming underinsured. This is where the property value increases (due to market appreciation or improvements) but the policy's coverage ends up being significantly less than the new value of the property. If that happens, be ready to get an updated homeowner's insurance policy so that you can keep your property (and all of its value!) properly insured.

Contractors

If the property needs rehab, you should have contractors look at the property prior to closing as well. Not only will this give you a better idea of your actual construction budget going into the deal, it might open up opportunities to ask for credits at closing. Being able to present a contractor's quote for repairs can serve as proof that the credit you are asking for is legitimate, giving more leverage in negotiations.

Different jobs typically require different contractors. Many city codes require licensed contractors to work on certain parts of the building, like plumbing or electrical wiring. In other words, you cannot always (legally) hire an unlicensed handyman to install new plumbing in your building. Definitely check your local code.

So, be prepared to hire a separate contractor for your kitchen countertops, your bathroom, your floors, your paint, your roof, your HVAC, your electrical, your windows, and your foundation among many other things. Some contractors might be able to do a few of those things, but they will not necessarily do them all cost effectively. This will take a little bit of price shopping until you better understand market rates for different jobs. You might consider hiring a general contractor who will hire out sub-contractors him or herself to do the work. This will probably be more expensive but will take some of the stress out of searching for individual sub-contractors. Just make sure that your general contractor has a solid reputation!

Whether you use a general contractor or hire sub-contractors yourself, good contractors can be very difficult to find. This is where recommendations can prove especially valuable. A good contractor will be very careful about his or her reputation. A bad review from someone you trust is an especially dangerous sign.

You can start by asking your real estate agent for any recommendations. Just realize that an agent's brokerage might have some sort of agreement or partnership with a contractor to refer business, so make sure that this is disclosed beforehand. Friends and family who recently got work done on their homes are another good source. If you can find a local investor who has done rehabs in the past, he or she might be your best resource. Online forums and networking groups like *BiggerPockets* are a fantastic place for connecting with real estate investors throughout the country.

When you go into a rehab deal, carefully plan out a conservative budget for the rehab. Expect things to go over budget. You would never want to run out of cash for your rehab and have to leave a unit vacant for a few extra months because it isn't finished. That can be thousands of extra dollars down the drain if you are not careful. Hiring experienced contractors can help to eliminate some uncertainty, but no one ever really knows what will happen once walls and flooring start getting ripped apart. Be prepared for the worst.

But there is a lot of upside to doing a rehab. It's more capital intensive but you can multiply your equity many times over. Just realize when a rehab job is over your head. Everyone can probably handle some light, cosmetic rehab. But beware of "teardown" deals or complete gut rehabs without some significant experience or a lot of cash to burn.

Property Manager
This team member is technically optional, but critical for making your investment as passive as possible. Without a property manager, you will

have to manage the building yourself and deal with all tenant issues personally.

Property management can be a rough business. Property managers deal with peoples' homes on a daily basis. Tenants may exaggerate how bad something is in their space, or they might fail to notify a manager before a problem leads to larger damage. The first person to deal with an issue is the property manager, who largely gets the most emotional fervor from an angry, upset, or confused tenant.

This isn't to say that all tenants are bad. On the contrary, some tenants are a landlord's dream: they take care of the space they rent, do not disturb their neighbors, hardly complain, and pay rent on time every month. In fact, most tenants are like this. It's the small minority of tenants that cause most of the headaches for property managers and landlords.[4] That said, over the

---

[4] After working in property management for a couple of years, I only knew a small percentage of the tenants within the community. Of that small percentage, a smaller percentage consistently complained about little things and kept me and the rest of the team plenty busy all of the time. I've worked in 4 different apartment and condo communities, each of which had hundreds of units, and this extension of the 80 / 20 rule always rings true. That is, 20 percent of your tenants cause 80 percent of the problems, and 20 percent of

course of many years, a landlord will inevitably get at least one bad tenant.

The only option for a property manager is to act professionally in the face of an angry tenant, no matter how unreasonable that tenant. This is why it's imperative to find a patient yet punctual property manager if you do not choose to manage the building yourself.

It can be hard to flag down property manager recommendations. There is a lot of turnover in the industry because of the unique challenges it presents. Finding a veteran property manager is ideal, but even they will eventually retire. A younger person might switch careers. So, you should expect to eventually have to switch managers at least a few times over the many years you hold the building. Online reviews for property managers are quite helpful for seeing what their tenants think of them. Keep in mind that many reviews can be overly negative, but see if you can spot a trend.

Another way to "test" a property manager is to call their office at the number that tenants are supposed to contact. If no one picks up, that's a red flag. If you can't get a hold of someone within the

---

that 20 percent cause 80 percent of those problems, and so on.

same day, how is a tenant supposed to? There's no golden rule for vetting property managers, but try to put yourself in a potential tenant's shoes and see if the manager acts appropriately. Is the manager responsive? Is the manager polite?

Managing the building yourself is certainly doable. It just takes time, time that might not be worth the amount you would pay in property management fees if you turned it over.

Property managers are also a great resource for understanding market rents in your area. Before you close on the property, definitely run it by your would-be property manager and ask them for their opinion. See what the manager thinks the property can rent for and make sure it fits your projections. If it doesn't, then you might consider backing out of the deal. Not every property manager will manage any building you bring to them, so be sure that he or she would even manage the property in the first place! If a property manager is not willing to manage it, that could be another big red flag!

A Final Word on Building Your Real Estate Team
Real estate is not a solo game. There are a lot of moving parts to get a deal from start to finish. In order to succeed in buying your first

property, you cannot attempt to wear every hat. Let an expert handle each specific area and you will succeed.

That said, if someone is not performing well, you might opt to switch that person out. If someone else approaches you with his or her services and you trust him or her, you might want to find a way to adjust your team to make room.

Every member of your team should want to see you succeed. After all, it's in their best interests, too. Most of them only get paid if something closes. Certainly be conscious of their biases, but know that they will put in the effort to get you to the closing table after sorting through any obstacles.

Before you actually go on your property hunt, let's go over the special types of debt that make real estate investing especially lucrative over the long run.

Special Types of Debt for Real Estate
As I mentioned, real estate has access to some of the best financing available to anyone.

Owner-occupied loans are typically regulated and subsidized by the government. Or, more specifically, lenders are able to sell loans to the government when they meet certain standards, allowing lenders to take more risk. This makes them relatively cheap, but you have to jump through more hoops to get them. Most often, you have to live in the property for at least one year before you can rent out that particular unit. These loans almost exclusively apply to 1 to 4-unit buildings, since a building with 5 units or more is considered "commercial."

Wait a second, can't the government change the rules here, too? Yes, they certainly can. And they might make some sweeping changes in the future. But when you sign your loan, you enter a contract with the mortgage holder. The initial mortgage holder is typically a bank which creates the contract consistent with current regulations. The contract is then sold to someone else, either the government (via Fannie Mae and Freddie Mac, to name a couple giant government quasi-corporations) or to other banks, pension funds, and others. That mortgage holder is legally required to respect the contract, in the same way that you have to fulfill your obligations under the contract by making payments. Government regulations would change new loans, not ones that have already been memorialized via contract. If the government goes totalitarian and seizes property and nullifies existing mortgage notes, we will have much bigger problems on our hands.

Regardless, current mortgage loan offerings in the U.S. are some of the most favorable in the world. Let's go through some common loan types that can work well with the one property strategy.

Conventional loans are the most common type of owner-occupied mortgage loan. These loans conform with lending standards set forth by Fannie Mae or Freddie Mac, two large government-sponsored quasi-corporations that purchase many of these loans after the initial lenders close them. Conventional loans can require as little as 5 percent down on a property, and typically would never require more than 20 percent down.

FHA loans are an especially popular type of mortgage, tailor-made for first time homebuyers. The Federal Housing Administration sponsors this program, and its primary focus is allowing people to get into homes for very little down even if their credit or income situation is not the best. FHA loans require as little as 3.5 percent down. If your credit is very poor, you can generally still get approved for an FHA loan at 10 percent down.

VA loans, sponsored by the Department of Veterans Affairs, might be the most powerful real estate loan product on the planet. They let you buy a home without putting *anything* down. That's right, a 0 percent down payment. Unlike an FHA loan, which has a perpetual mortgage insurance fee, VA loans have no mortgage insurance to pay each month. However, you definitely have to earn the ability to qualify for VA loans; only former or active military members can get approved for them.

USDA loans, sponsored by the Department of Agriculture, are similar to FHA loans but are made for lower income buyers in rural areas. These loans allow someone who would otherwise fail to qualify for most mortgages to still have a chance of getting approved, assuming the person is buying in a rural area. While the USDA loan program is limited when compared to some of the others mentioned above, it can be useful in those specific circumstances.

Type	Description	Who Qualifies?
Conventional	• Offered by banks, credit unions, and other private lenders • Not directly guaranteed by the federal government but conform to Freddie Mac and Fannie Mae loan guidelines • Typically require at least 5% down • Rates depend on credit history and income among other criteria • Most common type of mortgage	• Depends on the lender's specific guidelines • Generally, anyone with solid credit and less than a 45% debt to income ratio, discussed later in this chapter.
FHA (Federal Housing Administration)	• Offer financing up to 96.5% of the value of the home (3.5% down) • Generally higher interest rates and fees than conventional loans, including mortgage insurance payments for the entire life of the loan	• Relaxed credit requirements • Loan limits depending on location of the home • Generally, those with less than a 45% debt to income ratio, but potentially higher.
VA (Veterans Affairs)	• Offer financing for up to 100% of the value of the home (0% down) • Lower interest rate and fees than conventional loans • No mortgage insurance fee	• Most active or former military members • Relaxed credit requirements • Loan limits depending on location of the home
USDA/RHS (United States Department of Agriculture / Rural Housing Service)	• Allow low to moderate income residents in rural areas to qualify for mortgages • Rates and limits depend on the area	• Lower income rural residents • People with income no greater than 115% of the adjusted area median income

Outside of government sponsored loan programs, there are many far less-regulated loan offerings out there. Adjustable rate mortgages, short-term loans with balloon payments after a few years, and many types of commercial financing can have significantly different terms than the loan programs we just went through.

While interest rates will typically be at least a couple of points higher than government-sponsored loans, private loans can still offer competitive rates that can make for lucrative real estate deals. Lenders can typically be pretty flexible with these loans, but the terms rarely will be as favorable as the government-sponsored loans. But you typically will not have to live in the property at all with unconventional loan products, so there's that.

Now is a good time to explain what a variable rate mortgage is and why you probably should avoid them for this long-term buy and hold strategy. A variable rate mortgage has an interest rate that changes periodically based on some pre-determined benchmark. Most often, this is the Federal Funds Rate or LIBOR, which are determined by bank exchange rates and central banks like the Federal Reserve, and both of which you have zero control over. Unlike a fixed-rate loan, where inflation and rising interest rates are your friend (since they make your fixed-rate loan relatively cheap), variable rate mortgages are exposed to lots of interest rate risks. If your mortgage starts off at 3 percent interest, but two years later it jumps up to 5 percent, your formerly cash flowing rental property might now be at risk of going negative.

The only time you would really want to consider a variable rate mortgage is if interest rates are already very high and seem like they will go lower in the near future. That way, your loan's interest rate will fall as well. However, as of the writing of this book and probably for the foreseeable future, interest rates are at rock bottom lows and probably will only go up, not down. This gives you an extra incentive to lock in a low interest rate with a fixed-rate loan, rather than risk losing your initial low rate to a future interest rate hike by something like the Federal Reserve. For a strategy spanning 30 years, interest rate risk is a real concern. It is practically eliminated with a fixed-rate loan when rates are as low as they currently are.

Whichever loan product you end up using, be sure to go over your options with at least a couple of loan officers at different banks or lenders. Even loans in the same program will have slightly different interest rates and fees across banks, so be sure to do some shopping between lenders at the very least!

Unless you are using a VA loan, chances are you are going to have to save up for a down payment. If this is your first real estate purchase ever, saving up can be intimidating. Let's go over some strategies for building your down payment now.

Saving Your Down Payment

Saving is the net of your income and expenses. It is nothing to be intimidated by, but it also deserves your attention. Besides good credit, solid saving practices are a must for making the one property strategy work well. If you are unable to save money, you may end up losing your property in foreclosure when you have no reserves to cover an emergency. If you don't know how to save, you can't build up your safety net. And without being able to save your down payment, there is no deal.

If you cannot save, you are not in a position to invest. You either are spending too much or are earning too little. Without a way to build up some initial capital, and without a way to avoid running into a future liquidity crisis, your finances are doomed. To start any venture, you will need money and a positive cash flow stream to maintain it. When cash flow is negative, as is the case when you are spending too much on avocado toast and coffee each month, your financial clock is ticking.

Think of your personal finances as their own sort of "business." You are in the business of living a fun life for as long as possible. You should naturally focus on long term "profits," or having the best, longest life possible. This can only be done by consistently bringing in money more often than it goes out, otherwise you risk starvation or being thrown into the streets! The profits you earn can be spent on doing other fun things or buying assets to increase your cash flow to then do bigger and better things that you want to do. If you cannot stabilize your own personal "business," what's showing that you can handle buying a property and servicing more debt?

But what's the best way to build up money? At the highest level, you have two options: bring in more money or send less out.

Saving money is entirely dependent on your grasp of your current personal financial picture. You must know how much you are bringing in and how much you are required to spend on necessary expenses. It is imperative to get on top of your personal finances should you have any chance of maintaining an inkling of stability.

Once you know what money is coming in and what money is flowing out, you can identify problem areas to fix. Maybe you are spending an exorbitant amount on weekend trips to the bar. Perhaps you are paying for a car that is too expensive for your ideal budget. Or maybe you eat out every day for lunch rather than taking advantage of drastically cheaper, homemade meals. Are you taking an Uber when you could just walk or hop on a much cheaper bus? Always be looking for sensible cuts to your budget. Reckless spending can be catastrophic to your investment strategy, so your expenditures must be carefully evaluated.

Those problem areas are not going to fix themselves. Once you identify them, you must act to remedy them. Certain habits may take months to break. Once you get the hang of things, however, your savings will continue to build. Discipline is the key to racking up your savings rate.

One very easy way to bump up savings is to take advantage of direct deposit tools at your job since just about every employer offers it. Rather than manually splitting your paycheck each month and risking the temptation of spending it on unnecessary things, let your employer send a portion of your check automatically to your down payment savings account. Then have the rest sent to any of your other accounts. This is what many call "paying yourself first." When you pay yourself first, you take the emotion out of having to save. Sock away something immediately, then you can use your discretion on the rest.

Do not let the temptation of having the money in your checking account mean that you should use your right to spend it on needless items. If you are serious about your goal of investing in real estate, or anything else, you should eliminate opportunities for waste. When the money is out of sight and out of mind, or at least thrown into a slightly harder to reach savings account that does not have a debit card attached to it, it is more isolated from any temptation you might have.

One great option for an investment savings account is a high interest account through an online bank like Ally, which typically offers a well above average interest rate. Because it's online, there are no physical locations where you can pull cash from. Your money is *slightly* harder to reach, and it can at least keep up with inflation in the meantime while you continue to save. When it comes time to make your property purchase, you can transfer it out of your account. Currently, Ally Bank accounts are free, so they are worth a look if you do not have one already. There are other, similar banks out there that offer free, high-yield savings accounts, ideal for parking cash for a down payment.

If you really want to remove any doubts that you will be able to use your savings before you are ready to invest, you can explore other products like CDs, which lock away your money for a set amount of time and give you (typically) slightly higher interest than a savings account. However, if an opportunity arises before your CD's maturity date, you may be out of luck since your capital will likely be trapped inside of the CD and not freely available.

You could also get more aggressive with your down payment savings and invest the money into other assets like stocks and bonds, but then you run a serious risk of short-term volatility. That is, you might watch your down payment money disappear in a market crash right as you need it. But you might also reach your savings goal much quicker. Consider your options carefully.

Long story short, set up your savings so that you can contribute to them automatically. You can't overthink something if there is no thought involved!

But what if you just cannot pay yourself first and have no money left over to save? The easiest way for just about anyone to increase their savings is to reduce their expenses. Reducing expenses is like an instant return on investment. If you were going to spend money on it anyways (housing, food, toiletries, etc.) why would you pass up an opportunity to discount it without losing much of anything in quality?

Some great ways to reduce your expenses are also fairly obvious. If you eat out a lot, opt to go to the grocery store and cook your own food. You might be shocked at how much you can save in a month just by cutting out two restaurant lunches each week and replacing them with far cheaper home cooked meals. Another way to cut expenses is to buy certain things that you know you will use in bulk, such as toiletries. Even Mark Cuban has advocated for buying toothpaste in bulk for this very reason. Online shopping can make this quite easy.

Other ways to save can be a bit more drastic. One of the largest expenses for most people is transit to and from work. If you finance a new car every two years and trade-in your previous one, consider holding onto your car for as long as possible rather than continuously eating the rapid depreciation that comes in the first couple of years of owning a new car. Or buy something that is a few years old already so that your payments can be much lower and you won't be facing big depreciation. Or, better yet, if you can find a way to utilize transit or even cheaper means to get to work, try that! If you can do it, moving closer to your work can save a lot on transit costs. Even if rent might be an additional $150 per month in the location closer to work, you can forgo having a car and can instead bike or walk to work, saving potentially hundreds each month. This can also save a lot of time each day from not having a long commute!

Speaking of housing, this often is the largest expense in anyone's budget. Finding ways to cut back on your housing expenses can free up a lot of cash to be saved and invested elsewhere, like real estate! If you live in the most expensive part of town, consider moving a few minutes away to save a couple hundred dollars per month on rent (assuming it doesn't drastically increase your transit costs). Depending on where you are living, just moving a few blocks away can make a massive difference in average rents. You can also consider splitting housing costs with a roommate, rather than paying for an entire unit yourself. It probably would be cheaper to split the cost of a two-bedroom versus having to pay the entire cost of a one-bedroom apartment. As always, take time to consider your options!

Cutting expenses creates instant savings. If you normally spend $1,750 per month on all of your expenses, and you can shave that number down to $1,500, that's an extra $250 each month that you can contribute towards your investment savings! And those $250 as part of a 5 percent down payment mean you can purchase an extra $5,000 in real estate every single month you can save it.

While it's unlikely that you have actually made your expenses as low as they can go, you can also attempt to increase savings by boosting income. This is certainly easier said than done, but there are a few ways to do this. Though it can be slower, one way to increase income is to ask for raises at your current job. Similarly, it might be advantageous to take a job at a different company for a similar role and use that opportunity to negotiate a higher initial salary at the new company. However, with salaried jobs, where you are trading your time for money, it usually is quite difficult to get any more than a 5 percent raise in any given year.

Instead, one way to dramatically increase earnings potential is to take a job with performance-based pay. In a performance-based job, you are paid for your results rather than your time. Income may be significantly less stable, especially when starting out, but there is no limit to the amount you can earn. You only have so much time in a day, so there is a physical limit to how much you can make with hourly wage jobs.

If you are especially passionate about real estate, it might make sense to look into starting as a real estate agent. Pay is based on the deals that you are able to close, plus you get to be around real estate all of the time. It can be a good way to earn money while simultaneously learning more about your own market. That's exactly why I got my real estate agent's license. However, to be a really good agent, you must work very hard and should be an expert in real estate. This is certainly achievable, and it's an option you should give serious thought to, assuming you are not an agent already!

Otherwise, there are many other commission-based jobs that pay you for your results. The key to success in any of them is to work hard and keep looking for ways to scale your earnings. It really is like building your own business rather than slowly crawling up someone else's corporate ladder. Definitely explore your options!

Also consider taking a look at some of the items you already have lying around that you no longer use or want. It is incredibly easy to sell something on Craigslist or Facebook Marketplace among dozens of other listing services. This can help you unlock a lot of new cash to prepare to invest.

Real estate is a capital-intensive industry. The purchase can cost you quite a bit of up-front money, even with a low-down payment loan, and unexpected maintenance issues can pop up from time to time. Before you get into a deal, it is imperative to have some reserves built up so that you are prepared to face a potential disaster.

Obviously, you need to have enough money for the down payment to purchase a property. You will also have to have a good amount to cover closing costs. If you plan to buy a dilapidated property, you will also need to be prepared to cover the rehab budget in cash. On top of that, you should have at least a few months of projected expenses saved up to cover future vacancies, maintenance, and capital expenses. If you are more risk averse, you can always bump up your reserves.

Technically, you can go into a deal without reserves covered. However, this leaves you with little to no room for error. If anything in the deal goes south, you might not have any cash to turn to. A couple of missed mortgage payments, an incomplete rehab project, and one vacant unit later, you will be well on your way to foreclosure assuming you did not have the cash to cover those expenses. You wouldn't want to lose a deal that you spent many months (or even years) saving for!

On a similar note, prepare yourself as though the deal is bad, even if it looks good on paper. You won't have to worry so much about a market turn, a rehab project that goes over budget, or an extra month of vacancy while you try to get your unit rented. These things happen to everyone, so do not pretend like they will never happen to you. Savings save deals!

Even if you get approved for a VA loan with a 0 percent down payment, you will still need to save up some money for closing costs and reserves. But how do you go about getting approved for a loan in the first place?

Getting Approved for a Mortgage Loan

There are two different ways to get a mortgage loan for real estate. One is in your own name, while the other is in an entity's name. An entity would be something like a limited liability company (LLC) that would own the property. LLC loans typically fall under commercial style financing which is more expensive and typically has harsher terms. LLC loans are less useful in the 1 to 4-unit range since you can already take advantage of the special owner-occupied loans mentioned previously. LLC loans are also harder to get, generally, since they depend on the property's "rentability" rather than your own income. This means that it will be hard to get a long-term loan on a property that needs any substantial rehab. It will also be tough when you do not have a track record to prove to the lender that you can handle the rental property game.

On the other hand, getting a mortgage in your own name is a lot more straight forward. It typically depends on your credit score and your current income. If those are both high enough, you can fairly easily get a 30-year, fixed-rate mortgage loan.

More specifically, to get approved for a loan in your name, you need to have a sufficient debt-to-income (DTI) ratio. Your DTI ratio is your total monthly obligations divided by your monthly income. It is similar to net worth expressed as a percentage, although it is admittedly not quite that simple. While net worth would count non-income producing assets, your DTI ratio only measures your total income as compared to your debt payments and other obligations. Your DTI ratio also only includes monthly payments, rather than total outstanding debt balances as with your net worth.

For example, let's say you make $36,000 per year, or $3,000 each month. You currently have a $150 car payment, an $800 mortgage payment, and a $50 credit card payment to make every month. Your total monthly debt payments are $1,000, so your debt to income ratio would be 33 percent, or $1,000 divided by $3,000.

Your debt-to-income ratio helps to identify your personal capacity for debt. Naturally, without more income, you would be unable to sustain a 110 percent DTI ratio. This would mean that you would be paying your entire monthly income and then some to cover your debts.

Typically, creditors look very closely at your DTI ratio before lending to you to make sure that you have plenty of room to cover your debts. While it is not a perfect measurement, it is a pretty strong indicator that helps creditors to avoid giving overly risky debt loads.

For most mortgages, lenders require your DTI (after including the potential mortgage) to be under 45 percent. Any mortgage that would put you above that will very likely be denied. Remember, lenders are taking a risk in lending to you. To mitigate their risk, they want to be sure that you have room to pay your loan even if your income drops significantly. When shopping for a property, calculate your maximum mortgage by multiplying your monthly income by 45 percent, minus your current monthly debt payments.

There are some lenders who will go above 45 percent DTI, but typically only for very high interest rate loans or those with rather unfavorable terms. Certain government insured loans (like FHA loans) can allow you to have around 50 percent DTI, in some cases, but come with higher fees and interest rates at the same time. Hard money lenders might be able to finance the property regardless of your DTI, but they will do so at an exorbitant interest rate or with very little time to pay the whole loan back (sometimes less than 12 months!). These loans have their purposes and can be utilized to your advantage, but they are not made for long-term deals on their own. You should probably focus on doing something with marginally less risk that is well within your financial means.

Thankfully, buying income producing properties allows you to decrease your DTI ratio. Lenders will typically let you count a certain percentage of the projected rental income on any extra units besides the one that you will be living in.

For example, let's say you make $48,000 per year. That comes out to $4,000 in pre-tax salary per month. You currently pay $200 per month in student loan payments, but you do not have any other debt or monthly obligations since you just finished school and live with your parents. Your debt to income ratio before the mortgage is a measly 4.1 percent. You find a quadruplex that you really like listed for $500,000.

You have enough money saved up to make a 10 percent down payment, so you would need a $450,000 mortgage. At 4 percent interest over a 30-year term, that means your monthly payment would be $2,150. Add on projected taxes and insurance and your total monthly mortgage payment would be about $2,500. If you were to take out a mortgage on those terms and add it to your monthly $200 student loan payments, you would have a DTI ratio of 67.5 percent, much too high to meet the 45 percent requirement. Looks like you're out of luck?

Fear not, your lender allows you to calculate the projected income for the other three units into your monthly income for DTI ratio purposes. Your lender projects that the other three units would rent for $950 each. They are allowing you to add 80 percent of the rental value of those three units, meaning you can add an additional $2,280 onto your projected monthly income. When you put your actual income together with your lender's projection, you now have $6,280 in monthly income on paper. Now, when you divide your $2,700 in projected monthly debt against your projected income of $6,280, your DTI ratio drops down to 43 percent. Looks like you are approved!

Well, almost. If you want the best loan terms, you are going to need to have a strong credit score, too.

Before we talk about credit scores, I do want to clarify that, with a $40,000 salary, it would likely be difficult to get approved for the 5% down mortgage in the example in this chapter. It would largely depend on the potential rents of the units that you won't be living in. If they are especially high, you'll be able to qualify for more loan. The rent yields on this property are fairly conservative. With the numbers assumed in this chapter, while also assuming that a lender takes 80% of market rents for DTI purposes, you'd have a monthly salary of $3,333 and rental income of $4,800 (3 times $2,000 times 80%). That means your total monthly income for DTI purposes would be about $8,100. The mortgage and PMI would be $5,000 per month in the example, which would put your DTI at 61%. You would not be approved at those numbers. You'd need a higher salary or higher rents to be approved. For simplicity, this example property is used consistently throughout this chapter without great alterations to the numbers since it still shows the power of the concept. However, the same principles apply if you end up using a $900,000 loan, or an $800,000 loan, and so on. If you can't get approved for a $950,000 mortgage on one property because rents or your salary are not high enough, you might find better luck with an $850,000 mortgage on a less expensive property with a slightly better rent yield. There are a lot of factors that determine whether you get approved for a loan, and realize that this one can change a lot from property to property. Anyways, let's talk about credit scores.

Your credit score is one of your most important personal financial measurements, especially if you are wanting to use a sizeable amount of debt to acquire real estate. Your credit score, which is also called your FICO score, is a number ranging between 300 and 850. The higher the number, the greater the likelihood that banks will be willing to lend to you because you are seen as a responsible borrower. The lower the number, the more lenders will see you as a bigger risk. Ultimately, lending is a people business, and banks typically will not lend to people who are measured unfavorably compared to the bank's standards, at least not on favorable terms.

What makes up your FICO score? There are 5 main categories that factor into your score.[5]

---

[5] myFICO. *What's in my FICO Scores?*. https://www.myfico.com/credit-education/whats-in-your-credit-score

FICO SCORE BREAKDOWN

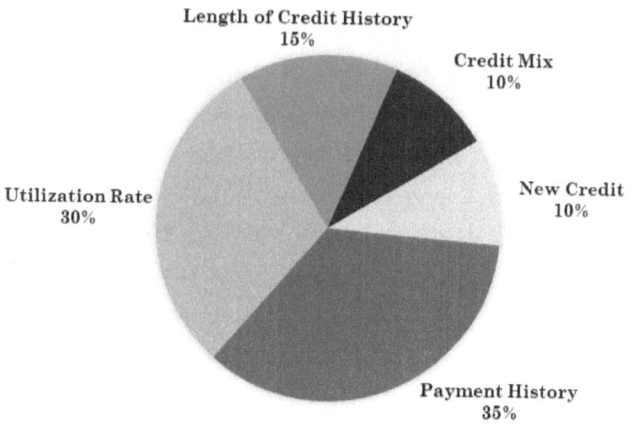

The largest contributing factor is your payment history. Quite simply, your payment history identifies whether or not you have missed payments and if you are consistently paying on time. Being the largest contributing category, it is imperative to make all debt payments on time or else your score could see huge negative drops, even from one accidentally missed payment.

The second largest contributing factor is the total amount of credit that you have available compared to what you owe, also known as your credit utilization rate. This measures how much of your credit that you are using in a given month. For example, if you have a credit card with a

$5,000 maximum limit and you carry a $1,000 balance, your utilization rate would be 20 percent. The lower your utilization rate, the better. Generally, a good rule of thumb is to keep your utilization rate under 10 percent, if possible. Otherwise, less than 30 percent should suffice. Increasing your available credit (be it from new lines of credit or increasing your existing limits) can push your utilization rate down, assuming you do not raise your spending with it. Opening new credit cards is a quick way to improve this category.

The third largest category is your length of credit history. This one, naturally, takes the most time to build up. You cannot go faster than time itself, unfortunately. Your length of credit history is just as it sounds; the longer you have held a certain line of credit, the higher your score. Closing old credit cards, for example, can ding your score significantly since it would lower your length of credit history.

The fourth and fifth largest categories are your credit mix and any new credit in your name. Your credit mix looks at the different types of loans that you currently have. Having a car loan and some credit cards might look better than just having credit cards and no other types of credit since it shows lenders that you can handle different types of debt. New credit, on the other hand, looks to see whether or not you have applied for new loans or lines of credit recently. Having a lot of inquiries into your credit within the last year or two can worry lenders into thinking that you are trying to get as much credit as possible very quickly, which can be an added risk in their eyes. A good rule of thumb is to avoid taking on more than 4 hard inquiries within any 12-month span. And definitely hold off from getting hard inquiries within a few months of applying for a mortgage. Hard inquiries drop off from your credit history officially after two years.

It is imperative that you take good care of your credit score. Without a decent score, it is unlikely that you will be able to get a large mortgage for a property. But what if you don't have any credit and, thus, no score? Let's take a look at some simple strategies to get the ball rolling so that you can have plenty of potential credit available by the time you are ready to purchase a property. Even if you already have a decent credit score, much of this information might still prove useful.

Building credit from scratch can be difficult without consistent, W-2 income, unless you already have a few years of 1099 income or commission-based salary history. If you can show a creditor that you have consistent income and no debt, you can rather easily get something like a credit card. Granted, the limit on the card will probably be very small to start, but it will be a way to get your foot in the door. To apply for a credit card, it will likely be best to go to whichever bank you use (preferably one of the bigger banks since they often offer solid introductory offers) and apply for one of their basic credit cards.

If you do not have a lot of income history or are worried about being unable to get a traditional credit card, look into taking out a secured credit card. This is where you give the bank a deposit to use as collateral for a credit card. Since the bank is secured by the money that you deposited with them for the card, they will almost certainly allow you to have a card since it's basically no risk to them. Use the credit card as you normally would and pay it off every month for a while. After a few months of building some basic credit history using your secured card, you can then apply for a typical unsecured credit card and continue working on building your score.

Carefully make sure to always pay off the balance each month. Lenders will see you as less of a risk if you show that you are responsible and pay off your debts without missing payments. Lenders do not want to have to deal with the high costs of default, so they try to make calculated decisions as far as who to lend to. Boosting your score can make their decision to lend to you that much easier, giving you much greater flexibility.

Credit card interest rates are relatively high. Missing payments can cost you a lot of money, not to mention the fact that you will lower your credit score and potentially miss out on getting the mortgage that you need to buy your property. At best, you will get worse terms on your mortgage because your credit score is lower than it would be otherwise, which will cost thousands over the life of the mortgage. Just a difference of .5 percent of interest on a $250,000, 30-year mortgage can cost you around $25,000 in extra interest over the life of the loan. A low credit score can come with huge costs.

With your credit score just up and running, it might take a little while to bring it up to the "very good" range (typically above 740) that will get you the best mortgage interest rates.

Hanging onto your oldest cards is a great way to help out your score. This one is easy since all you have to do is let time pass without closing the account. If you do not use one of your cards very often, be sure to use it at least once every few months to avoid having it closed, since banks and credit card companies might close a card if they see it is not being used.

Getting an additional credit card can help you to increase your score by increasing your credit limit (and thus your utilization rate) and your number of accounts. Even so, be careful not to get a bunch of new cards at once. Having lots of recent hard inquiries on your credit report can ding your score pretty significantly. Spacing out your credit applications so that you have at least a few months between each one can be a good strategy while you build your credit base.

The key to building and maintaining a good credit score is to be responsible. It's as simple as that. Pay off your credit cards each month by not spending more than you can afford. Pretend like the credit card is your own money, not someone else's, and you will be fine (it's only the bank's money for a month or so, then it becomes your bill). Setting up auto-payments to pay off your cards at the end of every month is a great way to avoid missing a payment. In time, once your credit builds over many years, you will unlock bigger and better offers with better rates, rewards, or other perks. Always be careful, regardless, as just one step too far can send everything toppling down. But it's easy to avoid that if you are cautious!

Prospective mortgage lenders will not like seeing hard pulls on your credit within 6 months of your proposed property purchase date. Generally, it is best to hold off on applying for new credit at least one year before you apply for your mortgage. That way your lender will not have any recent credit pulls to worry about.

Your credit score plays a big role in determining your interest rate on a mortgage. The higher your score, the lower your likely interest rate. A percentage point of interest on an $800,000 loan is going to sting, so get your score as high as possible before shopping for mortgages! If your score is below about 700, it is probably best to opt to try and raise it before locking yourself into a mortgage at a higher interest rate. However, as with any sort of investing or financial decisions, it entirely depends on your situation.

If you have taken large, non-mortgage loans out in the past and they are still unpaid, you may run into issues. Many Americans carry large amounts of student loan debt, for example. You may be one of them who has amassed six-figures of daunting student debt that is seemingly

128

unpayable. Depending on your current income levels, it may be necessary to first try and plow through that debt and pay it off before attempting to invest. Not only will it alleviate a huge amount of risk, it will bring your debt-to-income ratio significantly lower.

In sum, take your credit score seriously and do what you can to lower your DTI ratio to make room for a mortgage. With enough discipline, you will be in a position to finance your first property faster than you might think.

Fast forwarding a bit, when you are ready to shop for properties, make sure to get a pre-approval letter from your lender to show that you could get adequate financing on a particular property. This will also make your offer more competitive since you'll show the seller that you have all of your financing ready to go if the seller accepts your offer. After you get approved for a mortgage, you absolutely cannot apply for credit elsewhere without risking your approval. It is best to pretend that everything around you stops once you are approved for your mortgage until you close. In other words, do not go and apply for a $15,000 car loan when you are two weeks away from closing on your property. The underwriter in charge of your mortgage may be unable to allow you to get your property financed since your credit risk to them will have changed.

Remember, credit is a weapon, and it needs to be used with care. Lenders can get burned too when you burn yourself severely, so they will proceed with extra caution with most borrowers. If they are not too cautious in approving your application, beware of higher fees and interest rates that they will likely use to mitigate their risk.

With your team assembled, your down payment saved up, and your loan pre-approval letter in hand, you are well on your way to starting your property search!

Finding a Property
Before starting your search, it's critical to understand how to run the numbers on a property. It's very difficult to tell whether something is a good deal when you only know the purchase price. By running the numbers, you'll be able to see whether the property's rent will cover all of the expenses so that you can continue to advance with the one property strategy.

But how do you run the numbers? There are a few metrics that every buyer should be familiar with:

Metric	Formula	What does it do?
Net Operating Income (NOI)	Income – Vacancy Expense – Capital Expenditures Expense – Operating Expenses	This is your net income before you have to make any debt payments.
Capitalization Rate (Cap Rate)	NOI / Property Value	Gives you the return on the property assuming no debt is used.
Cash Flow	NOI – Debt Service	Your take home pay after all expenses and debt.
Cash on Cash Return	Cash Flow / Initial Cash Investment	The percentage of cash that you will get back based on your initial investment.
Return on Investment (ROI)	(Cash Flow + Mortgage Paydown + Appreciation) / Initial Cash Investment	The total percentage that your money will grow based on your initial investment.
Loan to Value Ratio (LTV)	Loan Amount / Property Value	The percentage of debt compared to the property's value.

These are not all of the potentially useful metrics out there.[6] However, this should be a great place to start for a basic rental property analysis.

In order to calculate these metrics, you first need to figure out a few things about the property. One is the property's price, which will be easy to get, and another is the total rent that it can bring in. You will also need to know what your mortgage, tax, insurance, and other expense payments will be on the property. You should also know what your approximate rehab budget will be, as that can be part of your "initial cash investment," which is a factor in many of the metrics listed above.

For example, the hypothetical property discussed at the beginning of this chapter had the following numbers:

Property Details	
Purchase Price	$1,000,000
Initial Cash Investment	$100,000
Total Rent:	$8,000

---

[6] For a free cheat sheet going over all of the major real estate metrics, check out the bonuses at the beginning of this book!

In this example, the net operating income (NOI) would be $8,000 minus $3,000 (total rent minus all non-debt expenses) or $5,000. This means the annual net operating income is $60,000. Your monthly debt paydown each month is $1,333, meaning it's about $16,000 during the first year. It doesn't cash flow since the debt payments eat up the remaining $5,000 in income not covered by expenses.

Metric	Formula
Net Operating Income (NOI)	$8,000 – $3,000 = $5,000 ($60,000 per year)
Capitalization Rate (Cap Rate)	$60,000 / $1,000,000 = 6%
Cash Flow	$5,000 – $5,000 = $0
Cash on Cash Return	$0 / $100,000 = $0
Return on Investment (ROI)	$16,000 / $100,000 = 16%
Loan to Value Ratio (LTV)	$950,000 / $1,000,000 = 95%

When you are running the numbers on a property, realize that no one metric is the "best." All of them have value in different ways. If you only looked at the cash on cash return on this property, you would ignore the strong ROI. Similarly, if you only looked at the strong ROI, you would ignore the fact that this property does not currently cash flow.

There are some rules of thumb to watch out for. For one, properties with a negative ROI should be a definite no-go. You'd be better off parking your money in a savings account making a tiny bit of interest over losing money in the deal. You should also aim to run numbers with a few different assumptions to see how different scenarios would play out: you can run one scenario with very low expenses, one with the likely expenses, and another with very high expenses. Try another projection where rent drops 5 percent. If a property still looks OK even with very high expenses and conservative assumptions, and even big rent drops, it's probably a strong deal.

You can use your cap rate as a rudimentary gauge to determine how reasonable your calculations are. For example, a cap rate over 20 percent is unlikely to happen on anything but properties in the highest risk areas with incredibly low prices. Conversely, you'd typically expect cap rates to be lower in more expensive, desirable areas (probably somewhere between 4 and 6 percent) since the deals are lower risk. So, if you're calculating a 15 percent cap rate when your market generally gets something like a 5 percent cap rate, check over your numbers and assumptions very thoroughly before moving forward. Similarly, a low cap rate in a less than desirable area probably means that the property is overpriced or has overly high expenses.

Understand the difference between cash on cash return and your return on investment. Return on investment includes things like appreciation and principal paydown, which you can only realize if you sell or otherwise pull money out of the property. This can be very useful in the long run but less so in the present. Cash flow, however, is money in your pocket each month. Cash flow is flexibility in the short-term. With a very high debt load (as with the example above), you'll likely see a big spread between cash on cash return and ROI because a lot of money will go towards your loan as principal paydown rather than to your pocket as cash flow.

Also keep in mind that these numbers will change over time. Your principal paydown will accelerate in a typical amortizing loan. Rent might increase as well. Conversely, you might have a large capital improvement that you didn't properly budget or build reserves for, and this can lower your return. In short, your metrics in year 1 will almost certainly be different than year 30. Because of accelerating principal paydown, the deal should get more and more lucrative, though that's no guarantee. To be safe, make sure that your deal works in year 1 in the event that you do not gain any appreciation or increased rent.

Run your numbers conservatively! If you are projecting a 30 percent rent increase after a couple of years, you are making a massive assumption. Always ask yourself if your numbers are reasonable. If they aren't, your metrics will be unreasonable as well, exposing yourself to unnecessary risk.

While you can manually crunch the numbers, it would speed up the process tremendously to create a spreadsheet using something like Excel or Google Sheets. Then you can just plug in the numbers for each deal and your spreadsheet will automatically calculate the metrics for you so you can see if it's a deal that makes sense. There are also templates online that can help you to get started.[7]

Now that you know how to do basic rental metrics calculations, you can start searching for properties. Not every area will be ideal for rental

---

[7] I have a free rental metrics calculator that you can use as a starting point — it's included in the bonus material linked at the beginning of this book!

property investing. Some areas have massive, seemingly illogical spreads between property values and rent values. Areas with low rent yields might be good for parking money, but would struggle to break-even every month without an especially large down payment.

If you are using owner-occupied financing, remember that you are going to have to live in this property for at least leave a unit vacant for about a year. This can complicate the search since your personal living standards might sway your investment decision. It is imperative to run the numbers on the property and understand whether it would serve your investment goal *before* ever becoming emotionally attached to it! Emotion can ruin this strategy, just as it ruins countless other investment plans.

Regardless, once you pick an area that (1) has a promising real estate market, and (2) you would be willing to live in, you can start searching in earnest. When I say a "promising" market, I mean one that has decent long-term projections. Ideally, this would be a growing area with a solid economic base. While you can make a more speculative investment, you increase your risk of losing out if the city goes under (look no further than much of Detroit in the 2000s). Chances are, there's a solid area within a 50-mile radius of where you are currently living. You do not need to find the world's best real estate deal – you just need something with decent fundamentals so you can build equity in the property without having a declining market take it all away.

Now would be a good time to acknowledge that not every area will have $1 million quadraplexes available. Some areas are wildly expensive, while others are comparatively cheap. If you are near an area with, say, $750,000 multi-unit properties, you can still make the one property strategy work for you. Even one $300,000 property purchase can dramatically improve your financial future if executed properly. The net result is still great, even if it might not be a particular benchmark (like $1 million) that you are aiming for. Who wouldn't want a paid off property heading into retirement? And, chances are, the cost of living in that area is probably lower as well, meaning that you would need less in retirement anyways, assuming you wanted to stay there.

Either way, look closely at the rental market in that same area that you are shopping in. Pretend that you wanted to rent a place in the area. See what apartments are renting for. Is there a lot of inventory? Do listings stay on the market for a long, long time? How do amenities affect rental values? You can really learn a lot about the local market just by browsing apartment listing websites.

Oftentimes, a multi-unit listing will show the projected rent of a unit. Do not trust this number. The seller has a vested interest in making that number look as high as possible – do your own research and see if similar units in the area are renting for that amount. If a unit is already occupied in the building, try to ask for more precise lease details earlier rather than later (i.e. when does the lease expire, what's the security deposit, etc.). If a unit's rent is much higher than typical market rents, that could be a major red flag. You'd hate to buy a property assuming that you could rent it for a certain price, only to watch the existing tenant leave and then being unable to rent it for that same price again.

Make sure you take unit quality into account when making rental projections. A unit that hasn't been updated in 25 years will almost certainly rent for less than a brand-new buildout. Maintenance costs might be higher on an older building as well. Will you have to update the units to bring them up to market rent? Or will you keep rents below market and lower your rehab costs?

Keep these considerations in mind as you search for your property.

Every property has a price where it will work as a rental. However, that price will be drastically lower than the current asking price in many cases, making a deal very unlikely. You have to remain disciplined and know what the break-even price on a property is based on your numbers. It's hard to undo an over-payment without big costs. If a property is listed for $725,000, and similar ones go for $700,000, the seller is probably just trying to get a little bit of extra profit and knows (or has a broker who knows) that it will probably sell for around market value at $700,000. On the contrary, if a home is listed for $800,000, but similar ones only go for around $600,000, you probably will have a tough time bringing the seller down to a reasonable number. That said, it can still be well worth shooting over an offer at a lower price to show the seller that you are interested. If they ever decide to lower the price, you will be first in line!

When you start your search, take a look at all available properties near your target price range and quality. This might be all multi-units between $700,000 and $1,000,000, needing no or little rehab. Then, systematically run the numbers on all of them and figure out what you would need the price on each to be for the rental metrics to work. Some properties might be listed at or near the price you need – focus on those first since other savvy buyers will see the same thing as you. Good deals come and go off the market very quickly; investors are always looking for them!

However, be very careful not to overbid. If a property has multiple prospective buyers, the seller will typically ask for a "highest and best" offer by a certain deadline. It can be easy to get carried away when you are so close to getting the property under contract. You must stay true to your numbers. It's better to lose out on a bad deal than to bid into one.

And stick to your strategy! You know what you want out of this deal, so make sure you can go and get it. It might take a lot of patience depending on your market, so be ready to get lots of offers rejected. Market conditions are always changing, so there's no telling what kinds of deals will be out there tomorrow.

In short, you have to be careful. This is easy to do once you understand basic real estate calculations and how to interpret metrics. To get comfortable with them, start running the numbers on properties in your current area, even if you are not ready to buy. You can only get better at running the numbers by actually running them. Then, once you are ready to buy, you can quickly and efficiently evaluate properties to see which ones are potentially great deals.

Buying the Property

When you actually find a property you want, you'll make an offer on it (through your agent) and hopefully will get it accepted. The other side might counter, but stick to your guns and know what price the property works at. Don't get emotional when negotiating!

Let's say your offer is accepted. Now you are "under contract." What does that mean? Simply put, getting a property under contract is when the buyer and seller agree on a price to go through with the sale and put it into a written contract. This contract is both sides' first line of defense against the other side backing out of the deal, depending on the circumstances. Getting a property under contract is like putting a fence around both parties, although just about any typical contract will have specific clauses allowing you to back out without penalty up to a certain date.

As exciting as it is to get a property under contract, there are still a number of steps to complete before it is finally yours.

Just about any deal will require a buyer to put up earnest money within the first few days of the contract period. Earnest money is typically just a way to show that you are serious as a buyer and that you will only back out for expressly contracted reasons during a specific time period, or else you will forfeit that earnest money. Earnest money is usually a small percentage of the selling price, and is submitted during the first few days of being under contract. If you make it to closing, the earnest money balance will get applied to your down payment.

Most often, on the residential side, the contract itself is a cookie-cutter template used for similar types of deals throughout your state, although you are free to use your own custom contracts. For residential deals, in many states, you get an attorney review period for a number of days after signing the contract. The attorney review period is the time that allows attorneys to take the initial sales contract and make edits that might be relevant to the specific deal or either client. It allows for addendums and concessions to be made as well before the contract essentially "locks in." These are often minimal edits in a straightforward residential deal. This review, or due diligence, period is the buyer's chance to have a professional inspection on the property done and back out if there is something that you might have missed in your initial walk through.

Naturally, to get an inspection done, you will need a licensed home inspector. As mentioned earlier, the value of a good home inspector more than pays for whatever fee he or she might charge. Not only can inspectors provide significant peace of mind in knowing that nothing appears to be wrong with the property (that's not already brought to your attention) they can help you to get significant concessions from the other side like credits at closing.

Don't hesitate to back out if something is revealed that would ruin the deal. Better to back out of a deal than to suffer through a bad one. The whole point of an inspection is to prevent buyer's remorse. Don't skip it! Whether you want to negotiate credits or not, an inspection should serve to eliminate uncertainty.

To get credits, the process is usually something like this: the buyer has his or her inspection done by a professional inspector, the inspector sends over a written report detailing the issues with the property, the buyer then forwards that along to his or her attorney or broker and then discusses what to ask for in concessions from the other side, and then both sides negotiate until an agreement is made. Some sellers will be much more open to credits than others, and it entirely depends on their motivations to sell.

Once any amendments, changes, or credits are added to your contract, you should be in fine shape for the rest of the deal. Obviously, this does depend on the contract that you and the seller signed. If it's a form contract, you almost certainly have the option to back out during the review period. After the review period, if you back out, it would have to be for a very specific reason, as outlined in the contract, or else you would have to surrender your earnest money or potentially be forced by a court to go through with a deal or pay some penalty.

The next couple of weeks after the initial review are generally used for officially securing financing. Your lender will send your mortgage file along to various teams to get your mortgage approved and ready for closing.

As discussed earlier, you will probably have to give your employment history, tax returns, current obligations, proof of insurance for this deal, and other personal details, assuming that you haven't already done that with your lender. They will have already pulled your credit score, most likely. Once they put together this package of information, they send it along to their underwriting team.

Underwriting is where mortgages are allowed to live or are selected to die. Although you will have a good idea for as to what your chances are for getting a mortgage, you technically never know until it gets through underwriting. But do not fret; if you have solid credentials, even as a first-time buyer, lenders are not in the business of denying people. They want you to succeed and recommend them for more business! They are only going to deny you if something significant comes up or if you are not cooperating with their instructions. If you have questions, be sure to ask them early and often!

Another critical step towards getting your mortgage approved is getting the property appraised. The lender will send out a third-party appraiser to determine the market value of the property. This will not necessarily be the buy price. Generally, the lender will use the lower number between the buy price and the market value as determined by the appraiser to calculate your loan-to-value number. This will determine if you have to pay for private mortgage insurance or if you get approved for the loan at all; if the mortgage would be for more than what the property is actually worth, the deal could fall through. Thankfully, this is very unlikely. Like underwriting, deals live and die at appraisal as well, though generally people are not buying for more than market value because buyers are the market!

Once a contract is signed, do NOT move large sums of money around without permission from your lender. You will have to explain to the bank where those funds are coming from, and it could kill the deal if they do not like an answer. Even more importantly, *never* take out new credit once the bank pulls your credit score. For the most part, you should not really be applying for new credit at all in the months leading up to your property hunt.

Of course, if underwriting denies your mortgage, it might throw you back to square one. Just about any sales contract will give an opt-out clause for not successfully securing financing, but you might have to forfeit your earnest money. If this happens, do a thorough investigation to see what it was that underwriting found or did not like. If you can fix it, do it quickly and try again! You might also consider going for a cheaper property and using less debt.

Assuming your property appraises high enough and you meet underwriting's standards, your lender will let you know that you are cleared to close, assuming the seller has done everything that he or she has been requested to do as well. Sometime around this point, you will receive your final mortgage details. You will know your exact rate, monthly payment, and any fees associated with your loan.

Now all you have to do is fund the rest of your deal, and you will be onto closing. Most often, this is done by wiring your down payment plus estimated closing costs to the title company that will be used for closing. Your lender or the title company holding the closing will give you specific instructions for sending over the money so that you are prepared to officially close.

Barring disaster, closing is the most exciting part of the deal. Both sides have had their teams work diligently to get to this point so that the property can finally be transferred. Most likely, both sides have provided everything needed to close well before the actual closing date.

Closing will most often take place at a title company's office. In most states, your attorney will have to present with you in order to close. If this is your first deal, however, even if you are in a state without the attorney requirement, you should definitely have your attorney at the closing table with you. The title company will have a designated person working on your file to make sure that they have everything that they need, while your attorney can walk you through all of the closing documents and spot any errors to be fixed.

In the days before closing, the title company should provide a final closing disclosure form which will show how much each side will owe or walk away with at the end of the deal. For the buyer, naturally, this number will typically be negative. This disclosure will show how exactly your money will be divided up on closing. There will be line items for lender fees, attorney fees, title fees, insurance premiums, your actual mortgage, your earnest money, and everything in-between. Although your attorney will review this document and should point out anything incorrect or missing, you definitely should double check it yourself and ask about anything that seems wrong. If you don't have an attorney, be extra thorough. Title companies definitely can make mistakes.

Before closing, you will also receive your final loan documents which show what your final payment and interest rate will be. For the most part, these will just be short, summary documents. The bulk of the lending documents will be reviewed alongside your attorney at the closing table. Your attorney will walk you through the details of the mortgage packet and explain what each document is signifying or doing. There will be a lot of them, especially with a government-conforming mortgage. If something is confusing, ask questions! But, hopefully, if your lender has been upfront and honest with you and you have been on the same page with them, there should not be any surprises here.

Buying a property is typically a person's largest purchase that they will ever make in their life, other than buying more real estate later on, potentially. It is incredibly easy to get anxious before, during, and after the process. The first wave of nervousness will likely come right as or after you get under contract. You will probably be wondering whether or not you are making the correct choice, whether the price is right, or whether or not real estate is for you. This is natural; if anything, it shows that you care!

When I went under contract on my first property, despite all of the excitement building up towards the deal and my years of educational preparation for it, I got very anxious wondering whether the deal was going to work. If you are anything like me, you will start going through hypotheticals like mad. What if I overpaid? What if I can't rent it out? What if I can't pay the mortgage? What if my credit gets ruined? It is not difficult to fall into this downward spiral of thinking. The first-time-buyer jitters are common. Focusing on your numbers can help to serve as reassurance – do not panic!

One of the great mindset shifts that many investors and entrepreneurs, in particular, make is realizing that any mistake or failure can be treated as "tuition" for learning how to better navigate something in the future. People pay sometimes hundreds of thousands of dollars for a degree, but everyone says that's fine, and they usually do not know how to buy property! The only failure would be not adjusting to avoid that same failure in the future! That said, unlike a degree, you can sell your property, even when it loses, say, 10% of its value. You can always sell in an emergency. Although there is debt on the asset, you still have a physical asset that you can sell, rent, or update to try and optimize the situation, no matter how poor it may seem. Although it is expensive, you do have some flexibility in how to go about making things better. You always have the ability to sell in a worst-case scenario. Of course, adequate reserves should prevent this situation, but you get the point.

All of that said, once you close on the property, your job is still not done. Now it's time to get the property rented!

Renting the Property
While most of the heavy lifting is done by the time you close, getting it rented is just as critical. If you are trying to make money with your property, your journey has only just begun, especially if you plan on holding it all the way until retirement.

Depending on your positioning, you will be subject to different rules and regulations. If you are an owner-occupant landlord, and the building is four units or less, you have a lot of flexibility in choosing a tenant because the Fair Housing Act probably does not apply to you, unless you list a room or unit with an agent or property manager. If you are renting out a home in which you are an absentee owner, you will have to be careful not to violate the Fair Housing Act.

The Fair Housing Act outlaws discriminating against prospective or current tenants based on race, color, religion, sex, disability status, national origin, and familial status. Some states also prevent discrimination based on sexual orientation as well, among other protected classes. Each state has their own set of housing laws as well, though most are sensible extensions of the federal Fair Housing Act. In other words, you cannot, as a landlord of rental property, deny someone from renting your unit because they are Jewish or because they are a different race than you. Either way, it is against your economic interest anyways to deny renters for arbitrary reasons like this. If you are trying to make money, turning away renters who are more than capable of paying rent with clean backgrounds is the equivalent of shooting yourself in the foot. And you'll be considered a jerk.

The Fair Housing Act also applies to rental advertisements. For example, you cannot put up a rental listing saying "Christians only" or anything discriminating against one of the protected classes. Similarly, you cannot say "Non-Married Couples

Pay Double" on your advertisement, since that's obvious discrimination as well.

That said, there are exceptions to the Fair Housing Act. It does not apply to owner-occupants of residential property (four units or less). In other words, if you theoretically wanted to prevent all people of a certain race from renting the other half of your duplex that you live in, you probably could. Again, it's definitely a poor business practice and could give you a pretty terrible reputation in the local community, but you could do it, technically. Of course, you should check your local housing laws before making any decisions like that. Then you'll be doubly encouraged not to do that.

Should you choose to make your own rental campaign after you move out, make sure to respect the Fair Housing Act and any local laws. You would hate to get in a lot of legal trouble right off the bat not long after closing on your property.

Renting out the unit yourself can be difficult. There's a reason that there are many people who make careers out of just being leasing agents. Not only do you have to market your unit, you will have to make sure your tenant is credit worthy and meets any standards set for your unit (that do not violate the law, of course), and then actually convince them to rent your unit.

Meanwhile, that prospective tenant will almost certainly be looking at a number of other units in the area, all offering something unique.

If you are showing your unit yourself, there are a number of steps that you can take to give yourself the highest chance of converting leads into tenants. First off, make sure the unit is clean! Add a subtle air freshener for showings as an added bonus. When you actually show the unit, turn on all of the lights and open up the blinds if it is a sunny day. You want the unit to be as well-lit as possible and as warm and inviting as you can make it. These little touches will help set you apart from other landlords who may neglect to take these easy steps.

When it comes to your actual "pitch," allow your prospective tenant to look around the unit themselves. If there is something that prospects totally have to see and you are not sure that they will find it, go ahead and guide them to it. Generally, if your unit is nicely maintained and is priced correctly, it will lease itself.

Self-listing your unit will take some time and effort, no doubt. However, it is important to know how to show a unit and what prospective tenants tend to look at when they are in a vacant unit. That way, if you ever chose to outsource the leasing and property management job to anyone else, you will know what talents to look for.

Should you choose to use an agent or property manager to list your unit, even if you live in part of the building, you will have to follow Fair Housing rules. That means you will have a lot less flexibility in arbitrarily choosing your next renter, but you won't have to spend the time in trying to lease it yourself.

Once the property is rented, and definitely after you move out of the property, you will be faced with the choice of continuing to manage it yourself or using a third-party property manager. Whichever you choose, be sure to weigh the costs and benefits of each to determine if it is the best for your situation!

It's probably a good idea to try leasing and managing the property yourself while you live in it if possible. This will let you better understand your property's quirks and any problem areas to take care of. Self-managing can be difficult, but, like leasing the unit yourself, can be very eye-opening to the struggles of property management and the key skills needed to do it right. That way, when it comes time to switch over to a property manager, you will know what to look for in your management candidates.

One of the keys to being a successful property manager is to set a strong precedent with your tenants as early as possible. You want your tenants to know that you are there to help if needed, but not to be their housekeeper. Laying the ground rules early and very clearly articulating what is and is not an actual emergency are good first steps. For example, you can emphasize that, in a unit with two bathrooms, a clogged toilet at 1 A.M. is not an emergency and can wait until the sun rises to be fixed. On the other hand, a leaking pipe is definitely something that should be addressed immediately to prevent further damage and increasingly expensive repairs. Explain this to your tenants right off the bat!

If you decide to go with a third-party property manager, this will take away most, if not all, of your interactions with tenants and can save a number of headaches. However, it is obviously not without a cost; often, you will have to pay a significant amount of your rent roll to a property manager. It typically is in the range of 8 to 10 percent of the rent roll depending on your market, plus any fees. And having a property manager does not necessarily mean that you will no longer be managing your property at all. Like communicating with your tenants, you should have an immediate conversation with your property manager to determine what does and what does not need your approval. You can determine a maintenance budget with your property manager up front and let him or her make a judgment call when problems arise, assuming they are not critical. In a best-case scenario, your property manager will be able to send quick updates on a weekly or monthly basis.

Realize that units will often need to be "turned" after a tenant moves out of them. This means that you will have to make repairs or otherwise spruce up the unit before re-renting it. This often includes new paint, carpeting or flooring, and smaller fixes, but they can get expensive. If a tenant has been living in a unit for years, there's a good chance that things will need to be replaced. This is why you have to maintain reserves (specifically for capital expenditures and vacancy) so that you can cover the cost of the rehab or repairs and your mortgage while the unit is empty.

Vacancy is a fact of life for landlords. You will inevitably have a month or two of lost rent and units that have to be turned. Unless you land absurdly loyal tenants, the chances of you never having any vacancy are slim. Prepare as though you will have to turn each unit in your property every year, just in case your tenants decide to move at the end of their leases. That way, you'll always have enough reserves to cover repairs and expenses.

Speaking of repairs and expenses, 30 years is a long time to maintain a property. The next section will go over some of the key things to watch out for when holding a property for the long haul.

Maintaining Your Property

Now your goal is to keep the property in good shape, fully rented, and insulated with reserves.

Let's talk about reserves, first. When you buy the property, you should have an initial amount of reserves saved up. That way, if your furnace blows out within your first month of closing the deal, you can have money ready to fix it quickly without having to scramble. You can also cover the mortgage for a few months if you lose your main source of income or the unit is vacant.

Reserves, in that way, are freedom. They are a finite amount of freedom, but freedom, nonetheless. Every month that you have rent coming in, you should be adding to this reserve pool. You should keep adding to it until you are comfortable.

In time, you will run into larger capital expenses. Buildings don't last forever without maintenance. Here are a few big-ticket items, and their estimated lifespans:

Item	Lifespan	Price
Roof	15 to 30 years	$8,000 - $20,000
Siding	50 to 75 years	$5,000 - $15,000
Furnace	15 to 20 years	$2,000 - $6,000
Water Heater	8 to 12 years	$1,000 - $3,000
Windows	15 to 40 years	$300 - $800 per window
AC Unit	15 to 20 years	$1,500 - $4,000
Plumbing	50 to 100+ years	$10,000+ (Varies)
Electrical	100 years+	$5,000+ (Varies)

Note that prices can vary for all of these projects as they depend on the age, size, and layout of the property. Climate can also be a major factor. But just one of these projects can throw a wrench into your finances if you do not have adequate reserves.

If you buy an older property, you might run into those larger capital expenses sooner rather than later. Old style galvanized plumbing, for example, doesn't do too well after about 75 years, and that can be an expensive job to replace all the pipes with PVC. Sure, the pipes themselves might be pretty cheap, but you have to rip up walls and potentially even dig into the ground to replace them depending on the severity of the issue. Realize that projects can get very expensive when you least expect them. The positive of doing a project like that is that you buy yourself many more years of (hopefully) no problems with that particular system. But, even then, there's no guarantee.

Always set aside a significant amount of the rent roll each month just for capital expenditures. Preventative maintenance and checkups can help to keep problems from escalating into nightmares, but you are definitely going to have some large projects down the line either way. Roofs don't last forever. Neither does a water heater. Don't get blindsided when these things need replacing!

When it comes to cosmetic upgrades, do pay attention to changing trends in your rental market. If you want to keep raising rents, you have to keep your units nice. However, dumping a ton of money each year into unnecessary upgrades is not what you should aim for; instead, pay attention to major trends and see if it makes sense financially to adopt them. For example, vinyl flooring is very "in" right now in most markets, replacing the tile and carpeting before it. Vinyl flooring might become old fashioned at some point, and some other type of flooring might take the lead years from now. To keep your unit at market rents, it might make sense to upgrade your flooring, though it entirely depends on your specific rental market. Just pay attention to see if there is something that you are falling behind in. A unit that hasn't been upgraded in 10 years will probably not rent for as much as one that was freshly renovated.

You can incorporate these sorts of projects into unit turns as well. That is, when a tenant moves out and something needs replacing anyways, you can upgrade it to fit with changing market tastes. If you keep enough reserves, you should be able to easily achieve this.

But if your tenants are very happy and you have very little vacancy, there might not be much advantage to upgrading the units. That said, it is still very important to check up on every unit even when they are occupied. This can take the form of a semi-annual inspection by you or your property manager, just checking to make sure that things aren't in disrepair. Then, if something needs repair or replacement, you'll know to fix it before it develops into a much larger problem.

If you take care of your property, it will take care of you. Some projects will be very expensive. Others won't be. It's best to be overprepared for them rather than unprepared. You'd hate to run into a liquidity crisis just because of a broken water heater.

Keep in mind, many of these projects are once-in-a-decade-type jobs. You aren't going to have to replace your furnace every year. But you should save up enough every year to be able to replace your furnace every ten years. The key is to spread out the cost of these projects over many months by saving for them in advance. It will be smooth sailing for the decades that you own the property if you do.

Putting It All Together

Let's recap all of the steps for executing the one property strategy.

First, you should figure out what your target area is going to be. Where are you planning on living? Does that area have good fundamentals, like a healthy economy and a growing population? If so, it's more likely to be a decent place for a long-term real estate investment.

You should then carefully construct your team. You'll need a real estate agent, lender, attorney, inspector, insurance agent, and any contractors for a potential rehab job. You should also vet a potential property manager if you do not want to self-manage.

Next, work with your lender to figure out what loan product is the best for you. Explain your strategy to them (i.e. how you want to live in one unit and rent out the others). Ideally, you'll be able to qualify for a fixed-rate, 30-year mortgage with a low down payment. This will also help for determining how much you are going to have to save to execute your strategy.

You'll have to save up for your down payment and your initial reserves, assuming you don't have the cash already. You should not invest in real estate without reserves. A good rule of thumb is to wait until you have a few months of reserves built up, if not 6 to 12 months' worth of reserves. That way, once you close on your deal, you'll have plenty of cash to subsist off of in the event that you cannot get it rented right away.

When you start searching for your property, carefully run the numbers on any deals that you are interested in. Every property could make a good rental, but only at the right price! Your job is to figure out what that right price is. Overpaying for a property can ruin the entire strategy. Stick to your numbers and make conservative assumptions. If the property would still work with those conservative assumptions, you've probably found a good one!

Once you get your offer accepted and go under contract, you'll have to send over your earnest money to the seller's agent or the title company. Meanwhile, have an inspector check out the property right away. If the inspector finds something bad that you didn't notice before, see if you can negotiate a credit with the seller. The credit can cover the cost to fix that issue, potentially, and the seller won't have to lose a worthy buyer.

If there is any rehab to be done, now would also be a good time to bring out any potential contractors to take a look at relevant portions of the property. If you know that one unit needs serious work in one of the bathrooms, bring out a contractor who can help with that and try to get a quote. By the time you close, you will be ready to go with your rehab since you will have all of your contractors lined up.

The lender will use the weeks leading up to closing to carefully vet your income history and credit report. They'll also send out an appraiser to make sure the property is worth what you are paying for it. Assuming everything checks out, you'll be well on your way towards closing the deal.

On the closing day, you'll sign any relevant documents (like the deed that actually transfers ownership of the property) and will officially transfer your money to the seller. You will only have to cover the down payment and your portion of the closing costs. Your lender will cover the rest of the purchase price.

After closing, it's time to get the property fixed up (if applicable) and then rented. If you have a rehab plan, now's the time to execute it. If the property is rent ready, you can spruce it up a bit and start marketing it for rent. You can do this yourself or use your property manager (or a third-party leasing agent). Every month that goes by without a tenant is another month of lost rent. But it often is better to get a solid tenant with good income history and credit after waiting a few extra weeks than to take a risk by bringing on a tenant with red flags. So do not rush when picking a tenant. Pricing your units slightly below market rent is a great way to get a lot of interest quickly, and then you'll likely have a greater selection of high-quality tenants to pick from.

After all of your units are rented, besides the one that you moved into yourself, you'll be well on your way towards retirement. Once you move out of the property and rent out that last unit, you'll have done the majority of the heavy lifting with this strategy. Now all you have to do is maintain healthy reserves and take care of your property for the long-haul.

Prepare yourself for big ticket capital expenses, like roof or furnace replacements. They will eventually happen, so set aside an appropriate amount of reserves each month to build a savings moat for the property. Similarly, always save some of the rent roll as vacancy reserves; that way, in the month that you have to turn and re-rent a unit after it goes vacant, you'll have some extra cash ready to go to cover expenses.

Every single month, your mortgage will be getting paid down, your net worth will grow, and you will be a step closer to financial freedom. Principal paydown on the mortgage will accelerate with each passing month, and you'll ideally get some rent and property value appreciation.

Do that for 30-ish years and you're done! If you make extra payments on your loan, you might be able to pay it off significantly quicker should you chose. Or you can choose to invest any extra income that you have somewhere else. The choice is yours. Speaking of choices, that is the subject of the final chapter of this book.

III. Creating Options

Once you buy your property, your retirement savings should be on autopilot. You have the flexibility to stop contributing to your IRA or 401(k) if you want to, assuming all goes well with your real estate deal. The one property strategy creates options. But what do you do with all of that freed up money and time?

1. Freeing Up Your Income

Remember the situation from the first chapter of this book? Where you were socking away $12,000 per year into your retirement accounts? That $12,000 is 30 percent of your $40,000 annual salary. If there are 250 workdays in a year, that's 75 days just towards retirement *every year*. Thirty years of that comes out to 2,250 workdays spent towards saving for retirement. That's over 6 years of your life.

But what happens when you use the one property strategy? Let's say you bought your property when you were 29. You live in the property for a year and move out afterwards, now at age 30. All of the property expenses are covered, you have reserves being replenished by the monthly rent, and a professional manager takes care of the day-to-day issues with the property. You just have to check in every now and then. You have 29 years left until the mortgage is paid off, which would make you 59 years old by the time your property can definitely fund your retirement.

Remember, the rental property is paying for itself at this point – you don't have to use your salary to make the debt payments. Every month, you gain equity in the property from debt paydown (plus any appreciation). If you land a really good deal or use less debt up front, you'll get some cash flow as well.

So, what do you do with the $12,000 that had been going into your retirement accounts? Well, you don't need it for retirement now. In fact, you can find a less taxing job (that happens to pay you less) if you really want to. If you no longer need to save those $12,000 for retirement, you don't need to earn them anymore either.

But the flip side is a viable option: why not invest your savings, too? Maybe you really like your $40,000 per year job and you want to supercharge your retirement saving. You still contribute everything you would have into your

Roth IRA and 401(k). Now, by the time you are 59, you will have *two* retirement nest eggs, one via your property and one via your retirement account holdings. You just bought yourself more security and flexibility in retirement.

You can also pay down the debt on the property more quickly. While this might not be the most efficient strategy from a return perspective (since you would be paying down low interest debt with money that could make a higher return elsewhere), it would unleash the property's cash flow much quicker. If your goal is early financial freedom rather than simply maximizing returns by the time you are much older, paying down debt can be a strong strategy. Paying down debt early is a sort of guaranteed "return" equal to the interest rate.

Simply put, you have real options for using your money. You can bump up your retirement savings or scale back. Whatever happens, so long as you maintain healthy reserves and keep paying off the loan each month, you should be gaining equity in your property and getting closer to unlocking all of that cash flow.

2. Risks of the One Property Strategy

Even though the one property strategy can be super effective, it is not without risks. If you truly rely on just the one property for your entire retirement nest egg, you are technically putting all of your eggs in one basket. If something were to happen to the property, all of your retirement income would be at risk.

This is why it is imperative to have sufficient reserves. The fewer investments you have outside of the one property, the more you should have in reserves. That way, if the rental income is interrupted for some reason, you still have money to live off of and cover expenses.

There is also a significant chance that the rental market in a particular area will shift for the worse at some point during the 30-year period and beyond. If you had bought a home in Detroit 30 years ago, you would have seen the city's economy decline precipitously decades later. Many homes in Detroit are still selling for only a few thousand each, some for far less.

While you can mitigate a lot of this risk by investing in an area with solid fundamentals (growing population, stable jobs, etc.), there is ultimately no telling where an area will be 30 to 50 years from now. Chances are that real estate will be more expensive many decades from now, but you never know.

Another risk is the one property strategy's reliance on debt. As discussed, debt is a double-edged sword. Not only does it increase potential returns dramatically, it increases risk too. This is because you are obligated to pay someone else. If you don't pay them, they get to take the property from you to satisfy the debt. This will wreck your investment and your credit score, so it will be hard to quickly recover.

The more debt you use, the more risk you are taking. Whenever you use debt, you have to be careful. That's why it's so important to have a solid reserve fund ready *before* jumping into any real estate investment. That way, if you lose rental income, have to repair the property, or upgrade it in some way to keep it marketable, you will have money ready to go and enough to cover debt payments for some time. If you think your reserve fund is too small, no one is stopping you from adding to it! Better to take a smaller return than lose the entire property. In short, tread carefully with debt.

There are also risks with legal liability when you have tenants. For example, if a tenant hurts themselves on your property because of some structural issue that you missed, they likely will come after you. If you own the property in your own name, it's imperative to have sufficient insurance to cover this sort of thing. You can even take out umbrella insurance to give yourself additional insurance coverage and peace of mind in case your homeowner's policy isn't enough. You can also beef up your homeowner's policy with a higher coverage amount.

You can also consider moving your property into an LLC or other liability-limiting entity. Definitely check with an attorney to see what that process would look like. However, LLCs and other entities are not indestructible – you can still be held personally liable if the court decides to ignore your entity, which it definitely can do if you do not very carefully follow the rules. Even if you do follow the rules, that is always a risk. So, plan on having great insurance in either case; it's well worth it. Not only will you potentially avoid financial disaster for yourself, but a person making a claim against you can still get adequately compensated through your policy if it's strong enough.

Even with these risks in mind, owning a rental property is still a fantastic way to build wealth with only a fraction of the initial investment when compared to other strategies. It's just important to realize what you are getting into before getting into it! There is always a risk of your investment failing, in any sector.

This is where diversification comes in. You can easily reduce your risk while using the one property strategy by diversifying your other assets. While your property is paying off its debt, you can focus on building a massive reserve fund with your freed-up salary. Maybe you can purchase stocks, bonds, gold, notes, and other assets to have some extra places to build wealth.

Diversification simply strengthens your overall foundation. If one investment fails, you have another to rely on. Similarly, if one investment is struggling, you have other investments to pick up the slack while you address any issues. It takes a lot of the pressure out of having to liquidate assets in a pinch, since you have other investments to buy you time.

The one property strategy creates options. The bulk, if not the entirety, of your retirement savings, are on autopilot. This leaves you, the real pilot, to focus on other goals. The more you can do to supplement the one property strategy, the more secure you will be financially. And, hopefully, it will be a lot easier to make progress than before, when you had the slow, uphill grind of parking a quarter of your salary into accounts you wouldn't touch until you were in your 60s. Better yet, maybe the one property strategy will get you more comfortable with the idea of purchasing a second rental property!

3. Adding a 2nd property

Because of its access to debt, buying rental real estate is a very scalable investment strategy. Once you move out of your first property, your debt to income ratio will likely go down. This is because you will have an extra unit's worth of rent coming in to add to your income. That means that you should be well-equipped to get approved for another mortgage, assuming your DTI ratio hasn't changed otherwise.

If you find that you really like real estate investing after doing one deal, what's the harm in doing one more? As long as you can keep a healthy reserve fund for each piece of real estate you own, you can keep buying real estate.

By just buying one additional property using another low interest, owner-occupied loan, you can double your eventual retirement nest egg. And then you won't be as exposed to the risks of something bad happening to one of the properties. Or maybe you just want to buy a smaller "back up" property that might not be able to fund your retirement on its own, but it can at least give you some supplemental income.

Similarly, if you want to make the one property strategy a two or three property strategy, that works too! That is, rather than buying one $1 million property, you buy two $500,000 properties. The net result would end up being practically the same — both properties would be fully paid off by the end of 30 years, and you'd get to keep the equity pool and cash flow.

Spreading your retirement nest egg across a few properties (especially in different markets) can be a great way to diversify your risk. If you have to move frequently to new cities because of your career, or if you just like to travel, you can try buying a new property in every city. Every time you move, just rent out your previous city's property so you can keep paying down its loan. If you do that three or four times throughout your career, you could build up a large net worth through real estate alone.

Just because it can't be stressed enough, whether you buy one property or several, it is critical to keep healthy reserves. Any amount of debt is a risk, after all, and you want to be able to cover operating expenses and the debt payment in the event that you lose rental income, even if only temporarily. Most failed real estate investors overleveraged themselves at some point and did not keep adequate reserves. They got too aggressive and stretched themselves too thin.

You are probably working with a very long investment time horizon, so you can afford to be patient here. If you aren't working with a long investment time horizon, buy and hold real estate probably isn't the best strategy. Generally, creating massive short-term returns would require more risk, like doing large rehab projects using lots of debt. Many investors do make a handsome living out of short-term strategies, but they are especially vulnerable to market swings, which do happen in real estate. When you invest for rental income rather than forced equity gain, market swings are typically less of an issue. But that can limit your upside too. It's a risk reward tradeoff.

Of course, if you don't want to expose yourself to real estate beyond a single property, that's fine, too. There are plenty of other investment options. The one property strategy is just one strategy of many. Let it be a foundation for you to explore other options later.

4. Flexibility to Focus on What Matters

Alternatively, if you decide that you'd rather work a less taxing job, you should be able to do that if you control your expenses. This is because you have $12,000 per year no longer needing to go towards an IRA or 401(k) to reach your retirement goals. The property takes care of that for you.

Even if you still decide to work at your current job to supplement your retirement fund, you can decide that you don't want or need that $12,000 in yearly earnings and instead take a job that pays you less but is less physically or mentally draining.

Whatever decision you make, your property should be on autopilot, paying down the mortgage each month and getting you closer towards a prosperous retirement. Adding to your retirement nest egg with your personal income will be optional. If you decide that you want to take on a higher paying, more difficult job again, you will not have sacrificed your retirement nest egg in coming to that decision.

But maybe you like your current job and would rather pursue opportunities at the firm you already work for. What to do with those $12,000?

Of course, you could always just invest the $12,000 into stocks, bonds, commodities, notes, and more real estate as discussed above. Accumulating diversified assets creates more options for the future and a stronger safety net in the event that something fails. When you're unsure of how to use the money, you might as well invest it and figure it out later!

You could also spend it on yourself now, rather than investing it for later. Those $12,000 would make for a handsome vacation fund, after all. Maybe you want to save up for a big purchase for your dream car. Or, far more altruistically, you can donate the money to your favorite charities (or start your own!).

Alternatively, you can take greater risks with the money to start a business or side-hustle to try and create an additional income stream. Cash is the lifeblood of any business, and you have more of it than you previously needed. Or maybe you've always wanted to throw down a big bet on high risk stock options to try and 10x your returns in a short period of time. Obviously understand the risks associated with whatever you decide to do, but enjoy the fact that you do not actually *need* this $12,000. That said, you can still use it productively and not recklessly if you so desire.

Just be careful not to stretch yourself too thin. Remember, no job is guaranteed. If you decide to finance a very expensive car and end up losing your job or you have to take a pay cut, you could find yourself in some serious trouble. The extra $12,000 is not an excuse to load up on bad debt.

To the contrary, you might opt to use the extra $12,000 to pay down any existing debts you have (besides the mortgage on the property). If you still have a car loan, student debt, or other debt not going towards an appreciating asset, you could focus all of your freed-up income on those loans. Then, when they are all paid off, you will have yet another level of financial flexibility and freedom. If you already don't have loans beyond the one property's, you could opt to expand your emergency and reserve funds. Now, if you end up losing your job or some significant portion of your rental income, you will have far less obligations to take care of and a heftier emergency fund to carry you through those months.

If you simply want to become debt free, you can throw all of your $12,000 at the property's mortgage each year. If you did that, your amortization schedule would look like this:

Amortization Schedules		
	No Extra Payment	Monthly Extra $1,000 Payment
Year 0	$950,000.00	$950,000.00
Year 1	$933,984.27	$921,747.74
Year 2	$917,274.45	$892,271.09
Year 3	$899,840.47	$861,516.98
Year 4	$881,650.94	$829,430.07
Year 5	$862,673.12	$795,952.58
Year 6	$842,872.84	**$761,024.26**
Year 7	$822,214.46	$724,582.22
Year 8	$800,660.80	$686,560.86
Year 9	**$778,173.05**	$646,891.75
Year 10	$754,710.73	$605,503.47
Year 11	$730,231.61	$562,321.51
Year 12	$704,691.61	$517,268.15
Year 13	$678,044.78	$470,262.27
Year 14	$650,243.13	$421,219.27
Year 15	$621,236.62	$370,050.86
Year 16	$590,973.03	$316,664.93
Year 17	$559,397.89	$260,965.37
Year 18	$526,454.36	$202,851.92
Year 19	$492,083.13	$142,219.96
Year 20	$456,222.33	$78,960.36
Year 21	$418,807.40	$12,959.23
Year 22	$379,770.99	$0.00
Year 23	$339,042.84	
Year 24	$296,549.62	
Year 25	$252,214.84	
Year 26	$205,958.69	
Year 27	$157,697.91	
Year 28	$107,345.62	
Year 29	$54,811.17	
Year 30	$0.00	

Note the bolded balances – in those years your PMI payment would drop off because your mortgage balance would have reached 78% of the original purchase price. That means that you would get at extra $4,800 per year from not having to pay PMI in year 6 when you make the extra payments as opposed to year 9 without them. More importantly, you pay off the property in its entirety eight to nine years earlier, unlocking your retirement income stream much quicker.

But is that really the best mathematical choice? If your mortgage loan has a low interest rate, probably not. If you only have to pay 3 or 4 percent per year in interest on the loan when you could simultaneously invest it to make 7 percent somewhere else (like the stock market), it technically makes more sense to invest that money. But this analysis ignores the liberating freedom of eliminating debt.

This choice to focus on paying off debt versus investing the money completely depends on your financial goals. Do you want to achieve early financial freedom? Or do you want to maximize long term returns? Both are great options, and there is no "right" answer as it depends on what you want.

And that's the beautiful thing about the one property strategy. You are leveraging other peoples' money to buy the property, and then other people pay the loan for you. You get to watch as your loan is paid down without having to contribute additional money to the deal. Your reserves should be increased every month and should cover any vacancies or repairs.

That gives you the flexibility to focus more on whatever else matters to you, rather than having to save a quarter of your annual salary for retirement. Whether that be your time (by reducing hours at work or taking a less taxing job) or other goals (like investing more aggressively elsewhere or starting a business) you have options. Let the one property strategy be the foundation for your financial future. You can build other things on top of it, but if those fall over you should still have your foundation to stand on.

5. One Property "X" Savings Strategy

Maybe you don't want to use the rental property for retirement, but you really like this premise of having someone else pay off debt on your behalf.

Let's say you just had a kid and plan on paying for their college 18 years from now. Given the massive costs of tuition, you assume that your child's college will cost $100,000 in today's money. How do you save up that money?

What if you took the one property college savings strategy? That is, you find a property worth at least $100,000 and finance it by using a 20% down payment loan. You have to fork over about $30,000 to purchase the property and setup reserves and all of that good stuff. If you can pay off the mortgage within the next 18 years, you will have a consistent revenue stream (to cover collegiate expenses) and a $100,000 property to sell if you'd rather take a lump sum. You can also take another loan out on the property to have your tenants pay for your kid's school by paying off *that* loan, too.

You have a couple of options to create a $100,000 equity pool in the property by the time your kid reaches college. You can stick with longer-term financing and pay at an accelerated rate to pay it off in 18 years rather than 25 or 30. However, a shorter mortgage typically comes with a lower interest rate. That means that you can probably get a 15-year mortgage on the property to save even more on interest costs. Keep in mind, you can always pay off a 30-year mortgage in 15 years, but you can't pay off a 15-year mortgage in 30 years. It might not be worth the slightly lower interest rate if you plan on trying to pay down the mortgage early anyways. However, if you find a property that cash flows really well, the property might be able to cover accelerated payments anyways.

The point is you can use the one property strategy to fund many different long-term goals. If you want to have a huge vacation reserve fund to take a lavish trip around the world, buy a rental property many years in advance and sell it once the loan is paid off and you're ready to travel (or hold it and use the rental income as a permanent "salary"). If you want to make a $500,000 donation to a charity at some point, buy a $500,000 property that has enough rental income to pay down the loan completely over time, and then sell that property to liquidate the equity into cash for your donation. This strategy is extremely useful for those sorts of long-term goals.

Postscript – The Wonders of Financial Independence

Ultimately, the one property strategy is just another tool to use towards financial independence. The one property strategy can replace your current retirement savings strategy, but it can also supplement it. Controlling more assets is rarely a bad thing, and it gives you flexibility to live the life you want in the good times and the bad. Nothing would stop you from buying additional property, or still investing a significant amount of money into the stock market, or working to build a business to create additional income. In fact, it's a smart move to diversify your investments and income streams.

Sadly, no one knows what the future holds. But you can take action to increase the likelihood that it is much more comfortable for you and your loved ones. If you never take action, you can be fairly certain that your future will not be much better than your present. Maybe that's fine with you, but I'm sure there's something in your life where having greater financial flexibility would help out a lot. And that can be well beyond your own worldly possessions – what if you could use all of your time to serve others because you built a fantastic future for yourself while you had the time and the energy?

Financial independence is not the exorbitance or pure laziness that it is often made out to be. Financially free people simply have options. They have the ability to scale back at their jobs. They have choice in how they structure their days. They have the ability to pursue new ventures. They own their time.

Now, some financially independent people take it many steps further to become massively wealthy for one reason or another, and some do live a life of total luxury. There is no shortage of get rich quick products promising this over-the-top lifestyle, where, for just a few quick payments of $999, you, too, can learn the secrets of success. But that is well beyond simple financial independence. Financial independence is security and freedom. You have greater freedom to become a wealthy goon if you so desire. After all, many millionaires and billionaires say that "the first million is the hardest." You can definitely step it up. But you don't have to, and that's a beautiful thing.

The one property strategy is simple, and it takes many years to bear fruit. It really is not special in itself. There are many ways to invest, and it's just one way. But the end result is just as sweet. You own your time, and you have options. And time is one of the truly finite things for each of us in this world.

Retirement is a different word for financial independence, and it can be achieved earlier rather than later if you so desire. Whether you realize it or not, unless you never plan on retiring at any age, your ultimate career goal is already financial independence. You know that you probably cannot work forever, so you build a nest egg over many years of commuting to and from your job. For many, by the time they are in their 60s, they reach some form of financial independence, even if it's partially supplemented by the government. This is "good enough" in the eyes of much of the population.

But, if you've read this far, you probably aren't satisfied with that path in some way. You want more freedom, or at least a more efficient route to it. I encourage you to continue educating yourself about saving, investing, and creating income streams. Valid strategies for achieving your financial goals exist, but they all have one common denominator: they all require your time and effort to get going. Whether that be investing a large sum of money at the beginning, a large portion of your time and effort, or some combination of both, no legitimate financial strategy avoids all risk or personal effort. And even the illegitimate one's risk dramatic punishments.

So, go forward with the knowledge you have and look to add to it. Sometimes that might mean taking bigger action; if you have read many books on buying rental properties, but have yet to buy one, you will learn a lot by actually going through with a deal. Learning by doing is significantly more effective, and any losses can be treated as tuition. Obviously, tread carefully, but not so carefully that you avoid acting altogether. With action, you can make real progress towards financial independence and beyond.

Acknowledgements

No one is self-made. I would not be where I am in my real estate career had it not been for the wealth of knowledge and support that I have received from countless others. Many of them helped me with this book. I'll take a moment to thank at least a few!

First and foremost, I thank my loving wife, EmilyAnn. She supports me through all of my ventures, no matter how wacky. I enjoy every day with her and look forward to a lifetime of those days.

Thank you to my parents for providing me with a stable household and upbringing while I was growing up, something that, unfortunately, many people do not get to enjoy. They continue to support me as I work my way through new challenges, and there is no way I could ever repay them for the positive impact that they have had on my life.

I'd like to thank my former college roommate and groomsmen, David Levering. We began immersing ourselves in personal finance and investing materials years ago, and we constantly explore new areas in finance together. We challenge each other's strategies and understanding as well, something even more valuable than simply sharing what we think we know. He helped tremendously with editing very early drafts of this book, helping me to fine tune material and clarify particular topics.

Thank you to my early readers group who helped me to finalize this book by offering valuable feedback. Their insights were critical for polishing the final draft!

And thank you to all of my subscribers on YouTube and blog followers who give so much meaning to the work that I do in creating new content and sharing information. Not only does the community motivate me to continue creating, but they often provide their own insight into my ongoing projects and offer useful, new perspectives. I am excited to see how the community grows in the future and the new value that it can create!

Download the Free Bonuses

Thanks for purchasing my book! To get access to all of the free stuff listed below, visit https://www.jackduffley.com/oprbook/.

- Rental Property Metrics Calculator
- Budgeting Spreadsheet
- Real Estate Metrics Cheatsheet

I also am a real estate agent in the Chicagoland area. If you are wanting to buy a property there, I'd be happy to help you, whether you are a complete beginner to real estate or a seasoned veteran. You can reach out to me directly by visiting http://jackduffleyagent.com/.

I'd greatly appreciate it if you left a review on Amazon! Your feedback will help others to discover this book and begin their paths towards building wealth in real estate.

Connect With Jack!

Find more content on real estate, personal finance, and other topics!

 Facebook: /jackduffley

 Instagram: @jackduffley

 Twitter: @JackDuffley

 LinkedIn: /in/jackduffley

www.jackduffley.com